THE ONLY WAY TO...
LEARN ABOUT HORARY AND ELECTIONAL ASTROLOGY

Also by ACS Publications

All About Astrology Series of booklets
The American Atlas, Expanded Fifth Edition: US Latitudes & Longitudes, Time Changes and Time Zones (Shanks)
The American Book of Tables (Michelsen)
The American Ephemeris Series 1901-2000
The American Ephemeris for the 20th Century [Noon or Midnight] 1900 to 2000, Revised Fifth Edition
The American Ephemeris for the 21st Century 2001-2050, Revised Second Edition
The American Heliocentric Ephemeris 1901-2000
The American Midpoint Ephemeris 1991-1995
The American Sidereal Ephemeris 1976-2000
Asteroid Goddesses: The Mythology, Psychology and Astrology of the Reemerging Feminine (George & Bloch)
Astro-Alchemy: Making the Most of Your Transits (Negus)
Astro Essentials: Planets in Signs, Houses & Aspects (Pottenger)
Astrological Games People Play (Ashman)
Astrological Insights into Personality (Lundsted)
Basic Astrology: A Guide for Teachers & Students (Negus)
Basic Astrology: A Workbook for Students (Negus)
The Book of Neptune (Waram)
The Changing Sky: A Practical Guide to the New Predictive Astrology (Forrest)
Complete Horoscope Interpretation: Putting Together Your Planetary Profile (Pottenger)
Cosmic Combinations: A Book of Astrological Exercises (Negus)
Dial Detective: Investigation with the 90° Dial (Simms)
Easy Tarot Guide (Masino)
Expanding Astrology's Universe (Dobyns)
Hands That Heal (Burns)
Healing with the Horoscope: A Guide To Counseling (Pottenger)
Houses of the Horoscope (Herbst)
The Inner Sky: The Dynamic New Astrology for Everyone (Forrest)
The International Atlas, Revised Third Edition: World Latitudes & Longitudes, Time Changes and Time Zones (Shanks)
The Koch Book of Tables (Michelsen)
Midpoints: Unleashing the Power of the Planets (Munkasey)
New Insights into Astrology (Press)
The Night Speaks: A Meditation on the Astrological Worldview (Forrest)
The Only Way to... Learn Astrology, Vols. I-V (March & McEvers)
    Volume I - Basic Principles
    Volume II - Math & Interpretation Techniques
    Volume III - Horoscope Analysis
    Volume IV- Learn About Tomorrow: Current Patterns
    Volume V - Learn About Relationships: Synastry Techniques
    Volume VI - Learn About Horary and Electional Astrology (*Available 5/94*)
Planetary Heredity (M. Gauquelin)
Planetary Planting (Riotte)
Planets in Solar Returns: A Yearly Guide for Transformation and Growth (Shea)
Planets in Work: A Complete Guide to Vocational Astrology (Binder)
Psychology of the Planets (F. Gauquelin)
Skymates: The Astrology of Love, Sex and Intimacy (S. & J. Forrest)
Spirit Guides: We Are Not Alone (Belhayes)
Tables of Planetary Phenomena (Michelsen)
Twelve Wings of the Eagle: Our Spiritual Evolution through the Ages of the Zodiac (Simms)
The Way of the Spirit: The Wisdom of the Ancient Nanina (Whiskers)

THE ONLY WAY TO . . .
LEARN ABOUT
HORARY AND
ELECTIONAL
ASTROLOGY
VOLUME VI

by MARION D. MARCH & JOAN McEVERS

International Standard Book Number 0-935127-29-1
Library of Congress Catalog Card Number 93-074600

Printed in the United States of America

Published by ACS Publications
5521 Ruffin Road
San Diego, CA 92123

First Printing, March 1994
Second Printing, January 1995

DEDICATION

To our beloved husbands, Nico March and Dean McEvers, who are loving and take pride in our accomplishments even though they still don't understand astrology.

TABLE OF CONTENTS

Index of Horoscopes in Volumes I, II, III, IV and V xvi
Introduction xxi

HORARY ASTROLOGY
by Joan McEvers

LESSON I   WHAT IS HORARY ASTROLOGY? 1

LESSON II   HORARY RULES & STRICTURES
         AGAINST JUDGMENT
         What Works and What Doesn't 4
         Strictures Against Judgment 8

LESSON III   THE HOUSES IN HORARY ASTROLOGY 10
         Directions as Indicated by the Houses 13

LESSON IV   THE PLANETS 14

LESSON V   TIMING 17
         More on Timing 20
         Answering Timing Questions 21

LESSON VI   RELATIONSHIP QUESTIONS
         Will He Marry Me? Does She Love Me? 25
         7th House Questions

LESSON VII   PURCHASES & SALES
         Will I Get My Dream House? 36

LESSON VIII   QUESTIONS ABOUT HEALTH
         Oh, My Aching Back! 42
         Other 6th House Questions
         All In A Day's Work 48

LESSON IX   OF KITH & KIN AND HERE & NOW
         3rd House Questions 52

LESSON X   FLY ME TO THE MOON
         9th House Questions 57

LESSON XI   AM I HAVING FUN YET?
         5th House Questions 61

LESSON XII   WHOSE MONEY IS IT, ANYWAY?
         2nd & 8th House Questions 68
         11th & 12th House Questions 76

LESSON XIII   WHERE DID I PUT IT? IT CAN'T BE LOST........ 78
             Finding Lost Items 78
             Lost Item Reference Table
             Signs... 82
             Houses.. 82
             Colors 84
             Charts to Learn From 85
             Missing People 90
LESSON XIV   COMPOUND AND MULTIPLE QUESTIONS
             Who, What, When, Where, Why and How? 95
             Other Considerations 98
LESSON XV   AND THE WINNER IS...
             Contest Charts 101
LESSON XVI   UNIVERSAL QUESTIONS
             Storms, Earthquakes and Wars 108
LESSON XVII "CLASSIC" HORARY CHARTS
             Yes, I Make Mistakes....................................... 111
LESSON XVIII QUESTIONS FOR YOU TO ANSWER
             Now the Reader Goes to Work 117

ELECTIONAL ASTROLOGY
by Marion D. March

LESSON I   WHAT IS IT?.. 131
             The Transcendentals 131
             Electional versus Natal Charts....................... 133
             The Philosophy of Electional Astrology 134
LESSON II   GENERAL RULES
             FOR ELECTIONAL CHARTS 135
LESSON III   MARRIAGE
             Tying the Knot 139
             Marriage Rules 139
             Tools of the Trade 140
             A Marriage Example 141
             More Wedding Chart Examples.................... 148
LESSON IV   MOVING INTO A HOUSE, APARTMENT
             OR CONDO
             Where You Hang Your Hat 156
LESSON V   BUYING OR SELLING PROPERTY
             (HOUSE OR LAND)
             Trading Places 161
             Rules for Election to Buy or Sell Property 161

LESSON VI   BUYING A CAR
                      Merrily We Roll Along 169

LESSON VII   STARTING A BUSINESS
                      Mind Your Own Business 174
                           Example Incorporation Chart 182
                           Rules for an Election Chart for an Organization 183

LESSON VIII   ELECTION FOR SURGERY
                      This is Your Life... 187

LESSON IX   OTHER ELECTION OPTIONS
                      Trips: On the Road Again 190
                           Lawsuits: To Sue or Not To Sue 191
                           Applying for a Job:
                           Work Makes the World Go Around 192

LESSON X   CONCEPTION AND FERTILITY ELECTIONS
                      Rock-a-bye Baby... 193
                           The Fertility Cycle... 193
                           Birth Control.. 194
                           The Best Time to Become Pregnant 194
                           Second Fertility Study.................................... 200
                           Pregnancies Through
                           New Medical Procedures 204
                                In Vitro Fertilization............................. 204
                                Artificial Insemination............................. 206
                           Fertility Practice Charts 210

LESSON XI   ODDS & ENDS 215

APPENDIX
                      PARTS OF CARS... 219
                      ANSWERS TO HORARY TEST QUESTIONS.... 220
                      ANSWERS TO ELECTIONAL
                      TEST QUESTIONS 223

Horary Astrology   by Joan McEvers

PAGE

Ex. Chart #1:   "Will the NFL go on strike?"   15
9 Sep 1987 9:20 pm PDT Coeur d'Alene, ID 47N41 116W46

Ex. Chart 2:   "Will I be safe if I go to San Francisco?"   16
11 Jul 1988 9:58 pm PDT Coeur d'Alene, ID 47N41 116W46

Ex. Chart #3:   "When will the Miltons buy my house?"   18
18 Oct 1992 12:55 pm PDT Coeur d'Alene, ID 47N41 116W46

Ex. Chart #4:   "When will we sell the house in Topanga Canyon?"   20
15 Aug 1985 3:19 pm PDT Los Angeles, CA 34N01 118W15

Ex. Chart #5:   "When will my business improve?"   22
31 May 1985 11:20 am PDT Coeur d'Alene, ID 47N41 116W46

Ex. Chart #6:   "Will we get the house in Fernan Village?
When will we find out?"   23
17 Aug 1979 8:49 pm PDT Coeur d'Alene, ID 47N41 116W46

Ex. Chart #7:   "Should I stay in San Francisco and work on my relationship?" 26
12 Nov 1992 8:40 pm PST Coeur d'Alene, ID 47N41 116W46

Ex. Chart #8:   "Should I use Connor as my attorney?"   27
3 Oct 1991 10:58 am PDT Coeur d' Alene, ID 47N41 116W46

Ex. Chart #9:   "Should I go into business with my brother?"   28
31 May 1985 7:55 am PDT Coeur d'Alene, ID 47N41 116W46

Ex. Chart #10:   "Is this relationship over?"   29
2 Jun 1991 9:46 am PDT Coeur d'Alene, ID 47N41 116W46

Ex. Chart #11:   "Will my son be okay if I let him go with his father?"   31
27 Nov 1985 9:08 am PST Los Angeles, CA 34N04 118W15

Ex. Chart #12:   "Should Steve hire Candy?"   32
5 Aug 1986 7:48 pm PDT Coeur d'Alene, Id 47N41 116W46

Ex. Chart # 13:   "Will my mother and brother be safe on their trip?"   33
13 Sep 1986 3:53 pm PDT Coeur d'Alene, ID 47N41 116W46

Ex. Chart # 14:   "Is this the right man for me?"   35
29 July 1985 5:30 pm PDT Coeur d'Alene, ID 47N41 116W46

Ex. Chart #15:   "Should we buy a new trailer hitch?"   38
25 Jun 1985 10:28am PDT Coeur d'Alene, ID 47N41 116W46

Ex. Chart #16:   "Will the Harrisons buy the house for $205,000?"   39
30 Apr 1985 11:45 am PDT Coeur d'Alene, ID 47N41 116W46

Ex. Chart #17:   "Is Mr. Moore going to buy the business Monday?"   40
5 Nov 1982 5:16 pm PST Coeur d'Alene, ID 47N41 116W46

Ex. Chart #18:   "Should I buy the tractor I looked at today?"   41
7 Jun 1990 2:51 pm PDT Coeur d'Alene, ID 47N41 116W46

Ex. Chart #19:   "Should I go to the doctor about my knee?"   43
23 Feb 1990 7:45 am PST Coeur d'Alene, ID 47N41 116W46

Ex. Chart #20:   "Will the biopsy find cancer?"   44
20 Sep 1985 11:50 pm PDT Los Angeles, CA 34N04 118W15

PAGE

Ex. Chart #21: "Am I allergic to the shampoo I am using?"   45
                28 Jan 1987 10:46 am PST Coeur d'Alene, ID 47N41 116W46

Ex. Chart #22: "Should I have a breast implant?"   46
                20 Jun 1987 6:26 pm PDT Coeur d'Alene, ID 47N41 116W46

Ex. Chart #23: "Will Mac ever walk again?"   47
                21 Oct 1985 11:53am MST Phoenix, AZ 33N27 112W04

Ex. Chart# 24: "Should I take the job at Shenanigan's (a restaurant)?"   48
                6 Mar 1990 8:47 pm PST Coeur d'Alene, ID 47N41 116W46

Ex. Chart #25: "Should I quit my current job and go into business with
                Miranda?"   49
                21 Jun 1985 12:15 pm PDT Coeur d'Alene, ID 47N41 116W46

Ex. Chart #26: "Will I get the job in Washington, D.C.?"   51
                28 Aug 1987 2:08 pm PDT Coeur d'Alene, ID 47N41 116W46

Ex. Chart #27: "Will I pass the real estate test tomorrow?"   53
                4 Apr 1980 1:48 pm PST Coeur d'Alene, ID 47N41 116W46

Ex. Chart #28: "Did a neighbor steal my money?"   54
                10 Dec 1986 9:04 pm PST Coeur d'Alene, ID 47N41 116W46

Ex. Chart #29: "Will the school levy pass?"   55
                2 Nov 1988 1:21 pm Coeur d'Alene, ID 47N41 116W46

Ex. Chart #30: "Is November 22nd a good day to defend my dissertation?"   56
                6 Nov 1985 3:10 pm PST Pullman, WA 46N44 117W10

Ex. Chart #31: "Should I go on Queen Elizabeth cruise?
                Can I afford it? Will I have fun?"   58
                5 Aug 1986 9:46 am PDT Coeur d'Alene, ID 47N41 116W46

Ex. Chart #32: "Will the court award supervised visits
                from my ex-husband to my daughter?"   59
                16 Jan 1989 7:47 pm PST Coeur d'Alene, ID 47N41 116W46

Ex. Chart #33: "How will everything turn out in court tomorrow
                with house in Montana?"   60
                24 Oct 1989 1:33 pm PDT Coeur d'Alene, ID 47N41 116W46

Ex. Chart #34: "Are we going to win Saturday?"   62
                22 Jun 1978 5:28 pm PDT Los Angeles, CA 34N04 118W15

Ex. Chart #35: "Should we buy Gold Cache stock?"   63
                26 Aug 1983 10:10 am PDT Coeur d'Alene, ID 47N41 116W46

Ex. Chart #36: "Am I pregnant? If so, will I have an abortion?"   64
                1 May 1974 9:40 pm PDT Los Angeles, CA 34N04 118W15

Ex. Chart #37: "Did my son start the fire?"   65
                27 Jun 1980 7:44 pm PDT Coeur d'Alene, ID 47N41 116W46

Ex. Chart #38: "Will Tim get custody of his kids?"   66
                7 Aug 1973 10:01 am PDT Los Angeles, CA 34N04 118W15

Ex. Chart #39: "Will my daughter have her baby while I am on vacation?"   67
                21 Aug 1986 11:32 am PDT Coeur d'Alene, ID 47N41 116W46

PAGE

Ex. Chart #40: "How long should I wait to implement the loan?"   69
1 Oct 1986 1:07 pm PDT Coeur d'Alene, ID 47N41 116W46

Ex. Chart #41: "Should I borrow money to buy more cows, rent pasture
and expand my operation?"   70
1 Jul 1990 10:55 am PDT Coeur d'Alene, ID 47N41 116W46

Ex. Chart #42: "Should my husband accept the settlement
from the insurance company?"   71
15 Mar 1990 9:13 am PST Coeur d'Alene, ID 47N41 116W46

Ex. Chart #43: "Will Tim get the loan to buy the house on 2nd Street?"   72
3 Jun 1990 7:17 pm PDT Coeur d'Alene, ID 47N41 116W46

Ex. Chart #44: "Is it safe to have sex with Leon?"   73
25 Aug 1990 8:49 am PDT Coeur d'Alene, ID 47N41 116W46

Ex. Chart #45: "Will Leon send me the money he owes me?
Will he come to see me? Will he contact me?"   74
16 Sep 1990 7:28 pm PDT Coeur d'Alene, ID 47N41 116W46

Ex. Chart #46: "Is this a good time to transfer my funds to a Swiss bank?" 75
27 Sep 1990 9:03 am PDT Coeur d'Alene, ID 47N41 116W46

Ex. Chart #47: "Will my friend come to visit this summer?"   77
18 Jun 1979 10:15 am PDT Coeur d'Alene, ID 47N41 116W46

Ex. Chart #48: "Where is my sweater?"   80
20 Dec 1992 11:15 am PST Coeur d'Alene, ID 47N41 116W46

Ex. Chart #49: "Where is Jim's billfold?"   85
26 Aug 1984 3:25 pm PDT Coeur d'Alene, ID 47N41 116W46

Ex. Chart #50: "Where is my cat?"   86
4 Jan 1983 8:41 pm PST Las Vegas, NV 36N10 115W09

Ex. Chart # 51: "Where are my airline tickets?"   88
1 Mar 1981 8:00 pm PST Coeur d'Alene, ID 47N41 116W46

Ex. Chart #52: "Where is my coat?"   89
12 Mar 1982 2:12 pm PST Coeur d'Alene, ID 47N41 116W46

Ex. Chart #53: "Where is Karen?"   90
27 Oct 1988 11:32 am PDT Coeur d'Alene, ID 47N41 116W46

Ex. Chart #54: "Where is Millicent? If she's dead, where is her body?"   92
10 Feb 1981 4:11 pm PST Coeur d'Alene, ID 47N41 116W46

Ex. Chart #55: "When will Ginny be found or return?"   93
13 Oct 1984 5:11 pm PDT Coeur d'Alene, ID 47N41 116W46

Ex. Chart #56: "Should Pam and I become business partners?
Should my husband and I move to California?
Is it financially feasible?"   96
12 Jan 1990 6:27pm PST Coeur d'Alene, ID 47N41 116W46

Ex. Chart #57: "Should Ben go into the service?
Should we buy Nikki (horse)? Should we move to Boise?"   97
15 Aug 1985 1:50pm PDT Coeur d'Alene, ID 47N41 116W46

PAGE

Ex. Chart #58: "If Chris goes to trial will he win?"   99
20 Mar 1987 10:27 pm PST Coeur d'Alene, ID 47N41 116W46

Ex. Chart #59: "Will the Vandals win the playoff game?"   102
9 Mar 1982 7:38 pm PST Coeur d'Alene, ID 47N41 116W46

Ex. Chart #60: "Is Houston going to win tonight?"   103
4 Dec 1980 5:35 pm Coeur d'Alene, ID 47N41 116W46

Ex. Chart #61: "Will the Redskins win the Superbowl?"   104
22 Jan 1984 4:00 pm Kansas City, MO 39N06 94W35

Ex. Chart #62: "Will Dallas beat Houston?" "Will it snow tonight?"   105
22 Nov 1979 12:40pm PST Coeur d'Alene, ID 47N41 116W46

Ex. Chart #63: "Will the Russians come to the Olympics?"   108
8 May 1984 11:14 pm PDT Coeur d'Alene, ID 47N41 116W46

Ex. Chart #64: "Will Murchison get the Bunker Hill mine?"   109
12 Dec 1981 11:12 am PST Coeur d'Alene, ID 47N41 116W46

Ex. Chart # 65: "Where is my ring?"   112
7 Mar 1974 12:58 pm PDT Los Angeles, CA 34N04 118W15

Ex. Chart #66: "Where are Jan's winter coats?"   113
2 Aug 1979 3:09 pm PDT Coeur d'Alene, ID 47N41 116W46

Ex. Chart #67: "Will my house burn down by the end of this month?"   115
3 Feb 1974 3:59 pm PDT Los Angeles, CA 34N04 118W15

Ex. Chart #68: "Where are Rick's rings?"   116
12 Jul 1987 4:45 pm PDT Coeur d'Alene, ID 47N41 116W46

Test Chart # 1: "Should I build the houses for and with Garrick?"   118
20 May 1991 9:15 am PDT Coeur d'Alene, ID 47N41 116W46

Test Chart #2: "Will Jerry get out on bail?"   119
13 Jul 1988 7:37 pm PDT Coeur d'Alene, ID 47N41 116W46

Test Chart #3: "Am I going to lose my home?"   120
15 May 1984 7:55 pm PDT Coeur d'Alene, ID 47N41 116W46

Test Chart #4: "Will Pete get his truck back?"   121
16 Sep 1991 2:10 pm PDT Coeur d'Alene, ID 47N41 116W46

Test Chart #5: "Is Matt guilty of the hit-and-run accident?"   122
18 Jun 1975 10:27 pm PDT Canoga Park, CA 34N12 118W38

Test Chart # 6: "Will the insurance company sue me?
If so, will they win?"   123
19 Sep 1989 1:20 pm PDT Coeur d'Alene, ID 47N41 116W46

Test Chart #7: "Will my daughter-in-law be involved in a lawsuit?"   124
23 Apr 1991 3:27 pm PDT Coeur d'Alene, ID 47N41 116W46

Test Chart #8: "Should I hire Gretel?"   125
21 Sep 1992 6:14 pm PDT Coeur d'Alene, ID 47N41 116W46

Test Chart #9: "Should we buy the Osburn property?"   126
7 Jul 1992 1:30 am PDT Coeur d'Alene, ID 47N41 116W46

Test Chart #10: "Where is the headache medicine?"   127
13 Nov 1986 10:13 am PST Coeur d'Alene, ID 47N41 116W46

Electional Astrology by Marion D. March   PAGE

Ex. Chart #1:   Possible Wedding chart for Lis and Jim.   142
                 7 Jun 1992 2:00 pm PDT Los Angeles, CA 34N03 118W15

Ex. Chart #2:   Another proposed Wedding chart for Lis and Jim.   143
                 7 Jun 1992 3:30 pm PDT Los Angeles, CA 34N03 118W15

Ex. Chart #3:   A third proposed Wedding chart for Lis and Jim.   144
                 7 June 1992 5:00 pm PDT Los Angeles, CA 34N03 118W15

Ex. Chart #4:   A fourth proposed Wedding chart for Lis and Jim.   145
                 7 Jun 1992 6:00 pm PDT Los Angeles, CA 34N03 118W15

Ex. Chart #5:   Voila! The best possible Wedding chart for Lis and Jim.   146
                 5 Jun 1992 6:00 pm PDT Los Angeles, CA 34N03 118W15

Ex. Chart #6:   Wedding chart for Marianne and Fred.   147
                 7 Apr 1974 11:00 am PDT Encino, CA 34N10 118W30

Ex. Chart #7:   Wedding chart for Jan and Rob.   149
                 8 Jul 1978 12:15 pm AHST Wailua, HI 22N03 159W20

Ex. Chart # 8:   Wedding chart for Franca and Carl.   150
                 13 Jul 1990 7:00 am MEST Basel, SWTZ 47N33 7E35

Ex. Chart #9:   Proposed Wedding chart for Chris and Brett.   152
                 15 Sep 1973 7:00 pm PDT Tahoe City, NV 39N10 120W09

Ex. Chart #10:   The actual Wedding chart for Chris and Brett.   153
                 16 Sep 1973 3:45 pm PDT Tahoe City, NV 39N10 120W09

Ex. Chart #11:   Move into house.   155
                 3 Dec 1973 3:00 pm PST Los Angeles, CA 34N03 118W15

Ex. Chart #12:   Move into apartment.   157
                 15 Sep 1988 noon MSET Zurich, SWTZ 47N23 8E32

Ex. Chart #13:   Offer to buy a house.   161
                 9 Jan 1992 8:00 pm PST San Diego, CA 32N43 117W09

Ex. Chart #14:   Put house up for sale.   163
                 1 Mar 1974 8:45 pm PDT Van Nuys, CA 34N11 118W27

Ex. Chart #15:   Put property up for sale.   165
                 10 Mar 1990 4:35 pm PST Malibu, CA 34N04 118W43

Ex. Chart # 16: Buying new car.   168
                 1 Oct 1983 4:20 pm PDT Beverly Hills, CA 34N04 118W24

Ex. Chart #17:   Purchase of Rolls Royce.   170
                 15 Mar 1989 4:00 pm PST Los Angeles, CA 34N03 118W15

Ex. Chart #18:   Bookstore Opening.   175
                 16 Jun 1978 3:00 am EDT New York, NY 40N45 73W57

Ex. Chart #19:   Restaurant Opening.   177
                 1 Mar 1983 6:00 am PST Coeur d'Alene, ID 47N41 116W46

Ex. Chart #20:   Election for an incorporated organization.   180
                 28 Oct 1975 1:24 pm PST Encino, CA 34N10 118W30

PAGE

Ex. Chart #21:   Mindy – Natal Chart   194
                 6 Mar 1951 2:48 am PST Los Angeles, CA 34N04 188W15

Ex. Chart #22:   Mindy – Fertility Chart #1   195
                 24 Aug 1976 4:27 am MEDT (-2 Zone) Zurich, SWTZ 47N23 08E32

Ex. Chart #23:   Mindy – Fertilty Chart #2   195
                 22 Sep 1976 2:45 pm MEDT (-2 Zone) Zurich, SWTZ 47N23 08E32

Ex. Chart #24:   Mindy – Fertility Chart #3   197
                 21 Oct 1976 11:46 pm MET (-1 Zone) Zurich, SWTZ 47N23 08E32

Ex. Chart #25:   Marissa – Natal Chart   199
                 15 Jan 1951 1:20 am EET (-2 Zone) Athens, Greece 37N58 23E43

Ex. Chart #26:   Marissa – Fertility Chart #1   200
                 17 Oct 1980 3:47 am MET (-1 Zone) Monte Carlo, Monaco 43N45 07E25

Ex. Chart #27:   Marissa – Fertility Chart #2   201
                 17 Oct 1980 4:15 am MET (-1 Zone) Monte Carlo, Monaco 43N45 07E25

Ex. Chart #28:   Sarah – Natal Chart   203
                 10 Apr 1952 8:31 am EST Stamford, CT 41N03 73W32

Ex. Chart #29:   Sarah – Fertility Chart #1   203
                 17 Jun 1985 10:00 am EDT Hartford, CT 41N46 72W41

Ex. Chart #30:   Jennifer – Natal Chart   205
                 2 Jan 1954 7:09 pm PST Glendale, CA 34N09 118W15

Ex. Chart #31:   Jennifer – Artificial Insemination #1   205
                 12 Jul 1990 2:30 pm PDT Hollywood, CA 34N06 118W19

Ex. Chart #32:   Jennifer – Artificial Insemination #2   207
                 11 Oct 1991 8:45 am PDT Hollywood, CA 34N06 118W19

Ex. Chart #33:   Jennifer – Artificial Insemination #3   207
                 11 Oct 1991 3:30 pm PDT Hollywood, CA 34N06 118W19

Chart #34:   Mindy – Fertility Chart #1   209
                 30 Sep 1978 7:52 pm MEDT (-2 Zone) Zurich, SWTZ 47N23 08E32

Chart #35:   Mindy – Fertility Chart #2   209
                 30 Oct 1978 10:33 am MET (-1 Zone) Zurich, SWTZ 47N23 08E32

Chart #36:   Mindy – Fertility Chart #3   210
                 29 Nov 1978 0:56 am MET (-1 Zone) Zurich, SWTZ 47N23 08E32

Chart #37:   Mindy – Fertility Chart #4   210
                 28 Dec 1978 1:46 pm MET (-1 Zone) Zurich, SWTZ 47N23 08E32

Chart #38:   Mindy – Fertility Chart #5   211
                 27 Jan 1979 1:09 am MET (-1 Zone) Zurich, SWTZ 47N23 08E32

Chart #39:   Mindy – Fertility Chart #6   211
                 25 Feb 1979 11:22 am MET (-1 Zone) Zurich, SWTZ 47N23 08E32

Chart #40:   Mindy – Fertility Chart #7   212
                 26 Mar 1979 8:42 pm MET (-1 Zone) Zurich, SWTZ 47N23 08E32

INDEX OF HOROSCOPES IN VOLUMES I, II, III, IV AND V

Ali, Muhammad	I	280
Andrew, Duke of York	V	66
Anne, English princess	V	65
Asner, Ed	III	225
Astaire, Fred	V	139
Bailey, Pearl	III	101
Baker, Howard	II	72
Baldwin, Faith	III	102
Beatrix, Queen	II	83
Benny, Jack	II	57
Bergman, Ingrid	v	122
Blue, Vida	II	69
Brahms, Johannes	V	67
Brando, Marlon	II	89
Braun, Eva	V	106
Bridges, Jeff	V	55
Browning, Elizabeth Barrett	III	59
Browning, Robert	III; V	61; 24
Bruce, Lenny	II	123
Buck, Pearl	III	100
Caldwell, Erskine	III	23
Cannon, Dyan	V	29
Caroline, Princess of Monaco	V	42
Carter, Jimmy	V	57
Carter, Rosalynn	II	124
Chamberlain, Richard	II	122
Charles, Prince of Wales	V	131
Cher	IV; V	129; 12
Chopin, Frederic	II; V	115; 95
Claudel, Camille	V	20
Clavell, James	III	24
Cohen, Mickey	III	27
Cole, Natalie	V	53
Cosell, Howard	II	113
Diana, Princess of Wales	III; V	170; 131
Dickinson, Emily	II	82
Dietrich, Marlene	III	8
Disney, Walt	II	236
Douglas, Mike	II	67
Dylan, Bob	II	110
Eastwood, Clint	II	80
Eddy, Mary Baker	III	81

Einstein, Albert	III	52
Eisenhower, Alex	V	146
Eisenhower, John	V	146
Elizabeth II, Queen of England	III; V	227; 26
Fawcett, Farrah	II	238
Fellini, Frederico	III	108
Field, Sally	II	73
Fitzgerald, F. Scott	III; V	16; 28
Flynn, Errol	II	61
Fonda, Henry	V	16
Fonda, Jane	V	91
Fonda, Peter	V	50
Ford, Betty	IV; V	6; 126
Ford, Gerald	V	126
Ford, Steve	V	60
Fosse, Bob	V	193, 197, 202
Freud, Sigmund	II	124
Friedan, Betty	III	87
Gabor, Zsa Zsa	II	92
Gandhi, Indira	III	37
Gandhi, Mohandas	II	70
Garland, Judy	I; IV; V	288; 146; 101
Gershwin, George	III	34
Goldwyn, Samuel	II	64
Gonzales, Pancho	III	216
Grey, Joel	III	214
Grofe, Ferde	III	42
Hauptmann, Bruno	II	61
Hayes, Helen	III	63
Hearst, Patricia	II	63
Hefner, Hugh	III	69
Hemingway, Ernest	III;IV;V	140; 163; 154
Hemingway, Mary Welsh	V	154
Hesse, Hermann	II	31
Hitler, Adolf	II; V	59; 106
Hudson, Rock	IV	39
Hutton, Barbara	II	66
Ives, Burl	III	219
John Paul II, Pope	III	12
Keller, Helen	II	59
Kennedy, Caroline	V	37
Kennedy, Ethel	V	124
Kennedy, John F.	II; V	75; 17
Kennedy, Robert F.	V	124

Kennedy, Ted	II	73
Killy, Jean Claude	II	123
King, Coretta Scott	V	111, 159
King, Martin Luther	V	111,159
Kissinger, Henry	III; IV; V	92; 134; 9
Koufax, Sandy	III	53
Kubler-Ross, Elisabeth	III	67
Lawrence, T.E.	II	67
Leary, Timothy	II	64
Lindbergh, Anne Morrow	V	136
Lindbergh, Charles	II; V	78; 136
Loren, Sophia	V	39, 129
Luft, Lorna	V	45
MacDonald, John D.	III	79
Mancini, Henry	II	121
March, Marion D.	V	80
Margaret, English princess	V	5
Mathias, Bob	III	45
McEvers, Joan	V	80
Mead, Margaret	III	30
Mehta, Zubin	II	122
Midler, Bette	III	226
Miller, Henry	V	76
Minelli, Liza	V	7
Mitchell, John	III	14
Mondale, Walter (Fritz)	III	54
Monroe, Marilyn	III; V	111; 13
Mussolini, Benito	V	22
Namath, Joe	II	121
Nash, Graham	II	99
Nash, Ogden	II	72
Nehru, Jawaharlal	II	88
Newman, Paul	V	27
Nin, Anaïs	V	74
Nixon, Richard M.	V	146
Patton, George	II; III; V	86; 124; 10
Peck, Gregory	III	218
Philip, English prince	V	26
Picasso, Pablo	II	87
Picasso, Paloma	V	59
Poitier, Sidney	III	230
Polanski, Roman	III	71
Ponti, Carlo	V	129
Porter, Sylvia	III	77
Pyle, Ernie	II	57

Raitt, Bonnie	V	144
Raitt, John	V	144
Redford, Robert	III	221
Remarque, Erich Maria	III	20
Reynolds, Burt	III	229
Rodgers, Richard	III	90
Rogers, Ginger	V	139
Ronstadt, Linda	II	99
Rooney, Mickey	II	70
Roosevelt, Eleanor	III	110
Roosevelt, Franklin D.	I; IV	286; 160
Rossellini, Roberto	V	122
Rudolph, Wilma	III	40
Sand, George	V	94
Sarah, Duchess of York (Fergie)	V	90
Schumann, Clara	V	71
Schweitzer, Albert	II	85
Sinatra, Frank	II	75
Smith, Robyn	II	68
Spacek, Sissy	III	222
Stalin, Joseph	II	92
Stookey, Paul	V	187
Streisand, Barbra	II; III; V	79; 188; 6
Sutherland, Joan	II	34
Thatcher, Margaret	IV	208
Toscanini, Arturo	II	63
Travers, Mary	V	187
Turner, Ted	V	23
Utrillo, Maurice	V	142
Vadim, Roger	V	19
Valadon, Suzanne	V	142
van Gogh, Vincent	II; IV; V	66; 90; 93
van Gogh, Theodor	V	92
Verdon, Gwen	V	32,191,197,202
Vivekananda, Swami	III	11
Wagner, Robert	IV	187
Walters, Barbara	III	223
Welles, Orson	II; IV	81; 122
West, Anthony	V	48
Wood, Natalie	IV	185
Woodward, Joanne	V	27
Yarrow, Peter	V	187

Composite - Adolf Hitler & Benito Mussolini   V   172
Composite - Anaïs Nin & Henry Miller   V   184
Composite - Betty & Gerald Ford   V   171
Composite - Camille Claudel & Auguste Rodin   V   181
Composite - Cher & Sonny Bono   V   184
Composite - Clara Schumann & Johannes Brahms   V   168
Composite - Coretta & Martin Luther King   V   159
Composite - Ernest and Mary Welsh Hemingway   V   155
Composite - Ernest Hemingway & Max Perkins   V   174
Composite - George Patton & Erwin Rommel   V   166
Composite - George Sand & Frederic Chopin   V   177
Composite - Ginger Rogers & Fred Astaire   V   164
Composite - Gwen Verdon & Bob Fosse   V   197 & 202
Composite - Ingrid Bergman & Roberto Rossellini   V   181
Composite - Margaret Thatcher & John Major   V   169
Composite - Marilyn Monroe & Arthur Miller   V   181
Composite - Peter, Paul & Mary   V   187
Composite - Princess Diana & Prince Charles   V   176
Composite - Queen Elizabeth II & Prince Philip   V   161
Composite - Rachele & Benito Mussolini   V   158
Composite - Rosalynn & Jimmy Carter   V   163
Composite - Sophia Loren & Carlo Ponti   V   179
Composite - Vincent & Theodor van Gogh   V   161

INTRODUCTION

After much urging by our students, friends and clients, we sat down, much sooner than anticipated, to write another book in our *The Only Way To...* series. Our subjects are **Horary** and **Electional** Astrology.

A **Horary Astrology** chart is for a question posed at a particular moment in time; an **Electional Astrology** chart is a chosen particular moment in time to initiate a specific event. Both systems are based on very old, traditional astrological methods — yet, in actual practice, we found that both methods could be modernized and, in the case of Horary, streamlined. There is relatively little literature available on **Electional Astrology** and although there are some excellent **Horary Astrology** books on the market, none of them teaches the subject the way Joan does, in an easy, succinct manner, simplifying many of the complex rules.

For the first four or five years of our astrological study, we both avoided the Horary field like the plague. But, ever curious, Joan was intrigued by the idea that one could set up a chart for a specific moment with a question in mind and find an answer in that chart. She couldn't quite believe it and finally decided to take some classes and learn for herself. She also delved into all the important books on the subject, including Barbara Watters, Robert deLuce, Ivy Goldstein-Jacobson, Geraldine Davis, and of course, the old master, William Lilly. The more she read, the more convoluted it seemed, and the more complicated it became. But true to her fixed Aquarian Sun and Ascendant, Joan faithfully stuck it out and with the help and encouragement of Sharon Culbreth spent many hours answering questions for family and friends.

As she became a sought-after teacher and speaker, her clientele increased, and with it the **Horary** questions and the time to answer them. The more queries she responded to, the shorter and more correct were the answers. One day she suddenly realized that she had dropped half of the ancient rules or imperceptibly changed them, and unwittingly developed a streamlined, updated and very successful version of **Horary Astrology**.

Marion became interested in **Electional Astrology** fairly early in her studies, but since she specialized in humanistic and psychological consultations, few of her clients asked Electional questions and it took her some years to realize that her approach, though not as revolutionary as Joan's Horary, was generating some excellent results.

As in all our astrology books, we only teach and write from actual experience. This book, more than any of the others, is based on our own way of approaching the subject. Some of our esteemed colleagues may raise an eyebrow or two, since their methods may differ considerably from ours, but we can assure you that astrology is a symbolic language and that many different ways of practicing it can be successful. In all our writing, Joan in particular is a stickler for stripping things down to the bare bones while Marion expands and elaborates. This method of working contributes to our long-standing collaboration because each of us complements the other. Yet we both find that the simplest, most direct ways bring the best results. That is what we do in this book, share with you our unraveling of ancient astrological practices.

Please refer to the last pages of this book for information on additional reports and calculation services available from Astro Communications Services, Inc.

Take Stock

Reading a book is no different than embarking on any other project — you have certain expectations. We suggest that you write down what you think you will get out of reading *Volume VI* of *The Only Way* Series. When you have completed the book, refer back to your expectations and see how closely we were able to fulfill them. Once you have "taken stock," please take the time to complete, copy and return the survey form on page 230.

Although not necessary, it is suggested that you have a Basic Natal Chart available when you read *Volume VI* of *The Only Way* Series. This will allow you to maximize the benefits and reading enjoyment you will derive from this book.

If you don't have a Basic Natal Chart, see page 229, for instructions on just how to order one.

Expectations

HORARY ASTROLOGY

BY JOAN McEVERS

WHAT IS HORARY ASTROLOGY?

Horary Astrology is an amazing but simple tool. It answers any question a person cares to ask and is calculated for the moment the astrologer hears the query and understands what it is about. It deals most successfully with concrete, well-defined inquiries. If the question is hazy, ill-considered or improperly stated, it cannot be answered correctly.

The word horary means "of the hour" and in today's language identifies the moment in time when a question occurs to the querent.

If the question to be answered is vague, unformed, tongue-in-cheek or just for fun, it is better for you, the astrologer, not to even try to answer it. However, if the querent's question is sincere and arises from a need to know, the chart invariably reflects the question and provides an answer.

Horary Astrology dates back to at least 1647 when English astrologer William Lilly claimed, "If a proposition of any nature be made to any individual, about the result of which he is dubious...let him but note the hour and minute when it was first made and erect a Figure of the Heavens...and his doubt will be instantly resolved..."

However, the rules and strictures against judgment seemed to be much too complicated and, to me, too time-consuming. I am not saying that the old systems do not work. They do. But I am a very busy astrologer and use whatever tools are at hand to speed up the process. I would never go back to calculating charts by hand, now that I have a computer; consequently since I have developed a modern way of dealing with Horary Astrology, I cannot go back to the ancient methods that take so much longer to use.

This branch of astrology is rooted in antiquity and many astrologers still apply an antiquated approach even in this modern day and age. I have updated these ancient rules and my new method, which was evolved through trial and error and thousands of charts, is what I present in this book. I have found over the years that my greatest learning did not come from the wisdom of the ancients, but through understanding and applying planetary rulerships, and the intricate structures of the houses and their derivative meanings. Through my study of the above, I was able to place the question properly.

As in all our books, the information given here is totally based on actual practice. You, too, will learn even more if you practice what is in this book.

The primary rule in Horary Astrology (and there are many), is to be sure the question is clear in your mind and that you note the exact time it occurred to you, or if you are the astrologer, the exact time when you understood what your client asked. If you have been mulling over the situation for many hours or days, it may not be wise to pose a Horary question, unless you can pinpoint the exact moment you first conceived the idea. This is not to say that just because you have concern for a problem over a period of time, you cannot ask about it; just try to note the exact time the entire or precisely phrased question first formed in your consciousness.

As in all astrology, timing is of the essence.

Many astrologers who are new to Horary ask if there is a special way to erect the chart. The answer is "no." The chart is calculated for the time the question is asked. You are setting up a birth chart for the question. That is all there is to erecting a Horary chart. The answer lies in the chart and is achieved in a **direct** and **uncomplicated** way, another area where I differ from most astrologers.

Interpreting the Horary chart is not difficult, but it does take time to learn the various rules that apply. In modern natal astrology, we use a psychological, humanistic and, at times, philosophical or even spiritual approach. In assessing a natal chart and forecast, we know that free will plays a part and the individual has the option to use the drives symbolized by a planet's position, either positively or negatively. Not so with Horary. This branch of astrology, like Mundane, is very cut and dried. Black is black and white is white and there are no shades of gray. The malefic planets (Mars, Saturn, Pluto) are just that — negative, while the benefic planets (Venus, Jupiter, Sun) are just that — positive. The Moon, Mercury, Uranus and Neptune can be negative or positive, depending on the subject matter of the question as well as their aspects.

Ancient Horary Astrology provides many strictures (a term actually meaning restrictions) to be considered in judging this type of chart. Since these strictures go back to the Middle Ages, many modern astrologers, myself included, do not hold with all of them. This is discussed in greater detail later.

Do not let rules and regulations frighten you. Horary is a very useful type of astrology that can give you concise answers where other astrological methods may fail. This **"KISS"** syndrome (keep it simple, Simon) will serve you well, as will a lot of practice. I am sure that in a short while you will become a Horary aficionado, just as I have.

HORARY RULES & STRICTURES AGAINST JUDGMENT

WHAT WORKS AND WHAT DOESN'T

The following rules apply to all Horary charts.

1. Horary can answer almost any question you choose to pose, but it is wise from the beginning to ask them so they are simple to answer. **The more carefully formulated the question, the easier it is to find the answer in the chart.** Naturally those which require a "yes" or "no" reply are the easiest.

Example: "Should I advertise in the Sunday paper?"

More difficult are queries which ask for a choice.

Example: "Should I buy the Fiat or the Cadillac?"

a) It is possible to reply to several questions asked at the same time. "Should my daughter go to St. George's school? Will her grades improve? Will she be able to take the bus?" As long as the questions are all posed at the same time, the astrologer will be able to find all the answers in the chart. These are called **compound questions.**

b) Questions on different subjects may also be answered from the same chart. Example: "Will I find the ring I lost? Is this a good time for a trip to Europe?" As long as the inquiries are framed at the same time, they can all be determined from the same chart. These are referred to as **multiple questions.**

c) If you, as the astrologer, receive a question in the mail, be sure to use the time and coordinates for where you are when you read *and understand* the question. The same with your answering machine. **It is not the time the person calls with the question, but when you hear and understand it, that you should set up the Horary chart.**

Many Horary astrologers differ on this subject. Some feel it is more accurate to erect the chart for the time and place the querent thinks of the question. *I suggest that you try both methods and use the one that consistently works for you.* When I began to explore this area of astrology, I used the time and place when and where the client thought of the question and occasionally upon the questioner's (usually another astrologer) insistence I still do it that way. However, as time passed, I tried different ways of looking at the charts and have found through trial and error that using the time and place where I become aware of the question works best for me.

d) It is very important that the astrologer understand what it is the questioner wants to know. Do not be afraid to ask the querent for clarification of the question. Many times someone will ask about a job (6th house) when they really want to know about income (2nd house). **Be sure that you clearly understand the query.**

e) **It is vital to place the question into the correct house.** This is the crux of Horary Astrology: placing the question in the house where it belongs. If this is not done properly, there can be no valid answer.

2. The querent is always represented by the 1st house; its ruler places the questioner in the chart. Any planets in this house help to describe the person who asks the Horary question. This is also true of "we" questions.

Example: "Should we invest in mutual funds?"
This is a 1st house querent.

3. If the question pertains to another person, especially by name, that individual is represented by the 7th house.

Example: "Should Bill take the job he was offered?" Bill is shown by the sign on the 7th house, its ruler and any planets in that house. If, however, the person is **designated by relationship,** you must look to that particular relationship house. **Example:** "When will my daughter find a job?" You would start with the **5th house,** which represents your children.

Again, astrologers differ in this area. Some maintain that if you know the relationship between the questioner and the person asked about, you should place the question in the correct relationship house...ergo "Should Vince look for a job in another state?" I put Vince in the 7th house and proceed from there. Even though I know that Vince is the questioner's brother, to me when any person is called by name, I use the 7th house to represent him, not as in this case, the 3rd. *You may wish to put it in the 3rd house. In the beginning of your study of Horary, you should try all methods.* My only advice is that once you determine what works best for you, stick to that method. **Consistency breeds accuracy.**

4. If the ruler of the Ascendant (the querent) and the ruler of the house that represents the question aspect each other, the type of aspect shows the answer. Squares and oppositions say **NO**. Trines and sextiles indicate **YES**. Conjunctions to the Sun, Venus, Jupiter and often the Moon and Mercury are usually positive. Those to Mars, Saturn, Pluto and sometimes Uranus are generally negative. A quincunx indicates that circumstances will have to change before an answer is available. Use major aspects only (conjunction, sextile, square, trine, quincunx, opposition).

5. All aspects are only considered when *applying*. Past aspects indicate action that has occurred **before** the question was asked. Orbs as such do not exist in horary astrology. If an aspect is applying, it can be from 0° to 29°. An aspect continues until either planet exits from its current sign. Orbs can be used to decide timing issues, as is discussed in Lesson V.

6. The Moon is always considered the co-ruler of the question and should be used to confirm or verify the answer obtained from the action of the planets, but it does not supersede the answer obtained from judging the planets. The Moon also figures in the Translation and Collection of Light. If the Moon is carrying the light from one planet to another and it makes flowing aspects to both planets, it confirms a yes (and in some cases gives a positive answer). If, however, it is making difficult aspects to both planets, the reply would be negative. An example of Translation and Collection of light: The Moon at 6 Aries sextiles Mars at 11 Leo and then conjuncts Mercury at 16 Aries. The Moon carries the light from Mars to Mercury; technically Mars and Mercury make no aspect.

7. Saturn or Mars rising (in the first quadrant) confirms a NO answer. Conversely, Jupiter or Venus confirms a YES answer. Note the word "confirms." Venus rising does **not** give a yes answer, nor does Mars there give a **no** reply. These are confirming placements only. (This does not apply to Aries, Scorpio, Capricorn, Taurus, Libra or Sagittarius rising.) If Uranus is involved in the question, most often the reply will not turn out as given. Uranus seems to indicate inadvertent changes in the querent's attitude, so that the question asked is not always the one they want answered. Neptune rising often suggests that the querent is confused, distraught or in tears.

8. If Scorpio is involved in a Horary question, use Mars as the ruler for your first consideration. Pluto moves too slowly to be of much help. In 1992, for example, if Scorpio rises and designates the querent, Pluto can only be in the 12th or 1st houses, which really does not give enough latitude for an answer. Fast moving Mars can give much more information. **Aquarius** and **Pisces** are ruled by Uranus and Neptune respectively, and these planets work quite well in Horary Astrology, but you may want to use the old rulers, Saturn and Jupiter, as well when you are answering questions with these signs prominent.

9. **A major rule is to always *write down the approach you will take to answer the question*.** I write my path on the same paper where I note the question. If a client asks, "Should I retire from my job?" I note that the Ascendant ruler represents the querent, that his job is depicted by the ruler of the 6th and that because retirement, in essence, means staying at home, I would consider the 4th house, as well. With such an outline in front of you, you will rarely go wrong. Being misled into taking the wrong path can be a pitfall for the Horary astrologer. A person asks a question and a logical answer occurs to you, but the chart says quite the opposite. Sometimes it is hard to maintain your objectivity.

A client once called and asked if she should invite Diana to her party. This question did not seem to merit a serious answer. Since she left the message on my answering machine, I didn't know the details that led to the question. I fully expected the chart to say, "Of course, invite her to the party." But, it said exactly the opposite. Do not invite her. When I gave the answer to the client, I asked what had prompted the question. She told me that this woman was a shirttail relative and every time she came to a family gathering she created problems. The client's husband had said, "Just don't ask her to the party." They didn't and the querent let me know later it was the best get-together they ever had.

10. **One of the most significant Horary rules is: *When you have answered the question, don't say anything else*.** The planets involved in the designated houses are the only ones that apply to the question and the answer. You can undo yourself if you do not adhere to this rule.

Many Horary Astrologers pride themselves in their ability to describe what happened before, during and after the question. One of the reasons for my success in Horary interpretation is that I stick to the answer only. Nobody cares what color laces your grandmother had in her shoes last Tuesday. Just answer the question, no more, no less.

11. **Retrograde Motion.** Whenever I explain that we use **only** applying aspects in Horary Astrology (except those of less than one degree as explained later), the question of retrograde motion of the planets always comes up. Are the planets applying if they are retrograde? Theoretically they are not, but I find that in Horary charts they work as though they are applying. If the planet ruling any part of the question is retrograde, it sometimes delays the outcome. This is also true of an intercepted planet which can also delay action. As stated in the section

about lost items, if the significator is retrograde, it invariably indicates the article will be found, or the pet or person will return.

12. Planets in mutual reception reinforce a positive reply. Example: If Mars is in Taurus and Venus is in Aries and they rule the questioner and the question, this is a strong indication of a "yes" answer, if other factors in the chart support it. I do not necessarily feel that Mutual Receptions are strong enough to GIVE the answer without confirmation elsewhere.

13. Any planet in dignity or exaltation is strengthened in the interpretation of a Horary chart, while those in detriment or fall seem to work in a less positive way.

Often the Horary chart will mirror the question... a person asks about a job and the ruler of the Ascendant is in the 6th or 10th. This is comforting to the astrologer, but the chart is not wrong if it doesn't reflect the question so specifically.

14. Ancient rules also state that if a planet leaves the sign before the aspect forms, it is not applicable. I have not found this to be true. For example if the Moon is at 10 degrees of Aries and will square Mercury at 29 degrees of Cancer, I count that aspect although, in reality, Mercury will move into Leo before the Moon gets to 29 Aries.

15. The Nodes do not seem to apply in Horary Astrology. I do not use them; I have tried to see their significance in Horary, but find they have no impact. You, however, may want to consider them.

Strictures Against Judgement

These strictures are based on ancient rules which denied answers to questions. I have not always found that they apply, but you can and should judge for yourself.

1. 0 to 3 degrees rising sometimes indicates that the question has been asked too early, but I have found that it does not prohibit an answer.

2. With a late degree (27 to 29) on the Ascendant, the decision may have already been made or the question already answered. Again, it does not deny an answer, but may indicate a way out if an answer is not available.

3. Old rules indicate that you should not answer the question if the Moon is **Void of Course** (not making any major aspect before it leaves the sign it is in). I have found you may still answer, but a VOC Moon usually indicates there is nothing to worry about or that nothing much will come of the question. Sometimes, you do not need to refer to the Moon in answering the query, so it does not matter if it is VOC. Even though the Moon co-rules the question, many times it does not rule any of the houses pertaining to the question; the answer is obtainable without referring to the Moon, thus it doesn't matter if it is VOC.

4. Ancient astrologers refused to judge the question if the Moon (and sometimes the Ascendant) were in the *Via Combusta*, which is the area from 15 degrees Libra to 15 degrees Scorpio. I have not found it significant to observe this particular stricture, but if you have difficulty with an answer, check it out.

5. If Saturn is in the 7th house, check your math and evaluation of the question. See if you have used the correct time zone, time, etc. This is an ancient stricture against judgment and still works in spite of the fact that most of us use computers. We can make errors when putting data into the machine, or the astrologer's judgment is faulty and the answer given may be incorrect.

Strictures are sometimes useful when the astrologer cannot find an answer in the chart. This happens; be prepared. It helps when you can fall back on the fact, for example, that early degrees rise, so perhaps the question has not fully formed in the querent's mind; or the Moon is void, so not much can be expected to happen; or late degrees are rising, so the questioner has already decided.

LESSON III
THE HOUSES IN HORARY ASTROLOGY

In Horary the houses play a key part in learning how to interpret the answer. If the question isn't assigned to the correct house, you cannot get a proper reply. This is extremely significant and the following descriptions will get you started and help you understand the principles involved. For more complete definitions, I recommend *The Rulership Book* by Rex Bills, *Horary Astrology* by Anthony Louis, *The Astrological Thesaurus, Book I Houses* by Michael Munkasey and Simmonite's *Horary Astrology* as excellent reference books for more encyclopedic indications of the house in which to place the question. Your astrological knowledge and common sense will do the rest.

It is also important for you to understand the derivative house system. It is well explained in Volume V of March/McEvers *The Only Way to... Learn Astrology.*

1st House:

This house represents the questioner and any planets in this house as well as its ruler indicate her/his state of mind. Uranus and Mars suggest agitation, anger or irritation. Neptune and the Moon denote a state of emotional confusion or frustration and maybe tears. If Venus or Jupiter is in the 1st house, the querent is usually cool, calm and in a happy frame of mind. Saturn, on the other hand, can indicate worry or anxiety. Questions concerning health, attitude and appearance are shown here...also paternal grandparents, the fifth child, the fourth partner.

Examples: "When will my health improve?" "Should I get a face lift? Is this a good time?" "If I go on a diet now, am I likely to lose weight?"

2nd House:

Any question pertaining to money, wealth, earning ability, loss or gain by prosperity or adversity, moveable goods and material possessions is answered by the 2nd house. It is most helpful in tracking down lost items since it represents your belongings. A lost book may be depicted by Mercury, which represents books, in or ruling the 2nd house. It is not necessary for the chart to mirror the question, but it often does and then you know you are on the right track. More about recovering lost items in Lesson VIII.

Examples: "Should I open a savings account?" "Should we buy a new refrigerator?" "Will my income improve by the end of the year?"

3rd House:

Answers to questions about elementary education, schools, communication, cars and short trips (short time or short distance), siblings, neighbors, shopping, reading materials or correspondence may be found here. Media questions may be assigned to this house. It represents children of friends and step-grandchildren. Questions about contracts and tests should be placed in this house.

Examples: "Will I pass the state board final test?" "Should I buy the car I looked at today?" "Will our neighbors go in with us on the cost of the new fence?"

4th House:

This house solves questions relating to all domestic affairs, home improvements, real estate and parents (especially the mother) and it represents the outcome of any question pertaining to the 1st house, and the 4th from any house will illustrate how an event will end. For example, the 4th from the 7th (marriage), the 10th, suggests how a partnership may end. The 4th house characterizes the kitchen, food, cooking, motels and hotels, building lots and immovable possessions.

Examples: "Should we buy the house we looked at today?" "Will my mother come to visit us for the holidays?" "Is it a good idea to add a room on to the house?"

5th House:

This is the house of courtship, children, gambling, speculation and all forms of entertainment. It answers questions pertaining to pregnancy, sports, lotteries, music, games and creativity. It also describes income from real estate (as the 2nd from the 4th), speculation, the stock market and romance.

Examples: "If I buy a lottery ticket, will I win the prize?" "Should I learn to play golf?" "Am I pregnant?"

6th House:

Your health is found in the 6th as well as in the 1st; also types of illness, work, employees, servants, tenants, co-workers, agents, conditions relating to employment, including job changes. Questions about small animals, pets, wardrobe, climate and weather are answered here. This house represents stores and storekeepers, diet and dietitians and maternal aunts and uncles.

Examples: "Will my dog be okay after I take him to the vet?" "Will it snow tonight?" "Will I get the job I applied for today?"

7th House:

The 7th house illustrates questions concerning marriage, lawsuits, partnerships (both business and personal). Adversaries, lawyers and doctors are found here, anyone you confront on a one-to-one basis. This house represents your second child, nephews and nieces and the maternal grandparents. It also designates the thief, murderer or perpetrator of any act. All questions relating to people you call by name are found in this house.

Examples: "Is Bill Smith the lawyer I should hire to defend me?" "Who stole my money?" "If I propose, will my lover marry me?"

8th House:

Questions about taxes, surgery and partner's assets are properly placed here. Also legacies, insurance matters, death and wills. It is the house of other people's money and belongings, so assign any questions pertaining to those factors to this area. For instance, if you ask "Where is Bob's wallet?" you would look to this house. Bob is represented by the 7th; his belongings (wallet) by the 8th. Any time you expect money from another person, this house comes into play.

Examples: "Will the Tuckers come up with enough money to buy my boat?" "Will the IRS audit my tax return this year?" "Will the bank okay my loan application?"

9th House:

This house rules long distance travel (by time and distance), advertising, publicity, visions, dreams, affairs of the church and expressions of opinion. In legal affairs this house represents the court. It identifies brothers and sisters-in-law, grandchildren, the third child, second partner, teaching and teachers, airplanes and ships (also space travel, if you ever run into a question about that). Foreigners, foreign places, colleges, universities, all institutions of higher learning are found here.

Examples: "Should I take the cruise to the Bahamas?" "Will the University accept my credentials?" "Will the court rule in our favor in the medical malpractice suit?"

10th House:

Questions concerning career, business, employer, status, prestige, reputation and acceptance by the public are all described by the 10th house. Anything pertaining to notoriety shows up here. This house usually pictures the father, the judge in court proceedings, parents-in-law and anyone in public you ask about.

Examples: "Is this an opportune time to change career direction?" "Will my boss okay my pay raise?" "Will the judge rule in my favor in the harassment case?"

I also assign queries that do not fit into other chart areas to this house such as: "Should I put in a gas furnace?" I could not think of any house relating to furnaces, so I used the 10th and the answer was correct. You may never run across a question that defies house placement, but if you do, try using the 10th house if you run out of other options.

11th House:

Questions pertaining to friends, acquaintances, adopted and stepchildren, income from business (2nd from the 10th), sons and daughters-in-law, organizations and clubs are the province of this house. Here you find answers about cooperation or the lack of it, social activities and goals.

Examples: "Will the Elks Club rent the hall to us?" "Will I be accepted into the sorority?" "Will the business take in enough money this year to allow us to open another store?"

12th House:

This house has to do with the past and often planets here indicate events that occurred before the question was asked. Enemies, secrets, plots, disappointments and sorrow are reflected here, as are institutions, hospitals and confinement of any kind. Questions about the partner's health, those connected with her/his job, large animals, zoos and scandal are judged from this house, as are inquiries pertaining to paternal aunts and uncles, sleep, sleepwalking, drugs, and drug dealers.

Examples: "Will my wife's health improve after she takes the treatments?" "Will my husband get the job he applied for?" "Should we buy the horse? Will it win?"

WHEN A QUESTION PERTAINS TO LOCATION THE HOUSES SHOW THE FOLLOWING DIRECTIONS

1st - East	7th - West
2nd- North by East	8th - South by West
3rd - Northeast	9th - Southwest
4th - North	10th - South
5th - North by West	11th - South by East
6th - Northwest	12th - Southeast

If someone asks where a lost object is and the significator is in the 6th house, you might suggest looking in a northwesterly direction. If a co-significator is in the 1st house, then you might say to look on the east wall of a room in the northwest area of the house...or the northwest corner of the east room.

LESSON IV
THE PLANETS

The planets obviously also have meaning when interpreting Horary questions. The placement of the question in the correct house is most important, but what if the question does not pertain to a specific house? "Will the hostages be freed?" was asked and I wasn't quite sure how to approach this question. If the querent had asked, "Will the hostages come home?" the question would have been much simpler. It would involve the 1st house (hostages) and the 4th (home). But where do we find freedom? I determined that both Jupiter and Uranus have to do with freedom and, in time, realized that the planetary significance is primary in placing the question properly. The following are other planetary associations that I have found useful: Mars and Uranus — accidents; Saturn — safety; Uranus — strikes; Neptune — leaks and lack of foundation; Pluto — tragedy. You, as you practice doing Horary charts, will find others. I have not found specific meanings for the Sun, Moon, Mercury or Venus other than the usual rulerships.

A few examples: A client once asked "Should we buy the house we looked at?" The rulers of the houses involved were in good aspect, but Neptune was in the 4th house, not very well aspected. I told her that before they bought the house, they should check the plumbing and foundation. Her husband did not "believe" in astrology, so they didn't follow through. A few months after they moved in, she called to tell me that the basement leaked and the foundation had to be shored up...and that her husband was impressed with astrology.

I have had several questions about strikes and could find no reference about which house strikes show up in. I used the 6th as the job and finally found that Uranus had impact in questions of this nature.

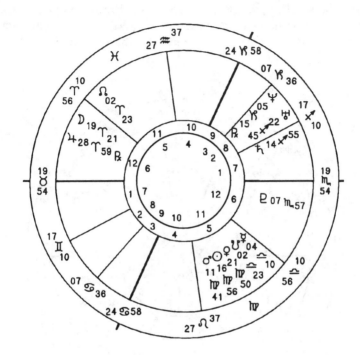

Example Chart #1:
9 Sept. 1987 9:20 PM PDT Coeur d'Alene, ID 47N41 116W46
"Will the NFL go on strike?"

The National Football League is signified by the 7th house which is
ruled by Mars at 11 Virgo in the 5th of the chart, which is the 11th
house of the NFL (counting from the 7th). The question basically asks if
they will stop working, which is a 6th house question. Since the question refers to the 7th house it is necessary to renumber the houses (see
chart). You can see that Mars also rules their 6th house of work (12th
house in chart). The Moon at 19 Aries, ruler of their 10th house (4th in
chart), and co-ruler of the question, makes no **applying** aspect to Mars.
Saturn at 14 Sagittarius is in their 1st house and will conjunct Uranus,
ruler of strikes at 22 Sagittarius. Since Saturn rules their 4th, it looks
as though they will be staying home, on strike (Saturn conjunct Uranus). Because their income would be affected, if we look at the 2nd house
of earnings, we find the ruler, Jupiter in their 6th house at 29 Aries
making no applying aspects (Void of Course) an indication of no action.
Both Uranus and Neptune are in their 2nd indicating a disruption in
their earning ability. They did go on strike for about three weeks.

When someone calls and asks about returning safely from a trip, or if their child will be safe in a given situation, Saturn plays a significant role. Saturn represents safety and if the aspects to Saturn are positive, it indicates that the trip will turn out all right, or that the child will be safe.

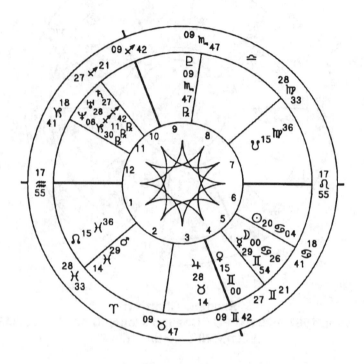

Example Chart 2:
11 Jul 1988 9:58 pm PDT Coeur d'Alene, ID 47N41 116W46
"Will I be safe if I go to San Francisco?"

A client called and asked this question; she was a very wary traveler and this trip was a challenge for her since she would be traveling alone, hence her apprehension. Uranus retrograde at 28 Sagittarius rules her. Mars and Pluto rule the 9th house...in her estimation it was a long trip...Mars at 29 Pisces is past the square to Uranus; Pluto at 9 Scorpio makes no aspect to her ruler. However, she did not ask IF she should take the trip, only if she would be safe. Since Saturn which is also retrograde at 27 Sagittarius is conjunct Uranus, I felt she would be safe. She went and had a rather uneventful — but completely safe — journey.

LESSON V

TIMING

Beyond doubt, this is the most difficult and frustrating part of Horary Astrology — at least from my point of view. The following is the method recommended by most texts, but I must say it is challenging at best and some of the time does not work.

This method claims that to time events the signs on the angles of the houses (1st, 4th, 7th and 10th) and the sign of the Moon must be considered.

CARDINAL signs are fastest:	Hours	Days	Weeks
MUTABLE signs are next fastest:	Days	Weeks	Months
FIXED signs are slowest:	Weeks	Months	Years

The houses must also be taken into consideration in timing.

ANGULAR houses relate to CARDINAL signs, so are the fastest.

CADENT houses relate to MUTABLE signs, so are next fastest.

SUCCEDENT houses relate to FIXED signs, so are slowest.

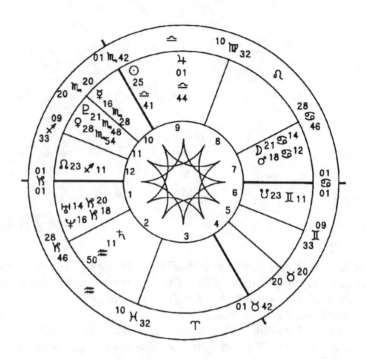

Example Chart #3:
18 Oct 1992 12:55 pm PDT Coeur d'Alene, ID 47N41 116W46
"When will the Miltons buy my house?"

The querent is represented by Saturn, ruler of the 1st at 11 Aquarius; their home is ruled by Venus at 28 Scorpio, since Taurus is on the cusp of the 4th; the Miltons are indicated by the Moon, at 21 Cancer ruling the 7th. The Moon will trine Venus in seven degrees approximately, suggesting the possibility of seven hours, days, or weeks. The Moon is in a cardinal sign and an angular house — according to our rules the fastest possible time. Venus, however, is in a fixed sign and a succedent house; that is the longest possible time, so is it weeks, months or years? We will discard the possibility of years. Most horary charts do not cover that span of time, unless the question specifically states the potential of an event taking years to occur.

We must check other areas in the chart for time measurements. There must be a connection between buyer and seller; the Moon (buyer) makes no aspect to Saturn (seller). So we must take into consideration other planets in the 1st and 7th houses. Uranus and Neptune are at 14 and 16 Capricorn in the 1st, the Moon and Mars are in the 7th at 21 and

18 Cancer. (The Moon and Mars move faster and are already past Uranus and Neptune.) There are no applying aspects between them. Let's check when the buyer's money (8th) will come to the seller (1st). Again the Moon which rules the buyer's 2nd (8th) makes no aspect to the planets representing the seller (1st). But the 8th house has Leo intercepted, so the Sun must be considered. There are no applying aspects between the Sun at 25 Libra and the seller. Looking for timing is the **only** time in Horary when you may use **past aspects.** There are 14 degrees between Saturn and the Sun, four degrees between Uranus and Mars, seven degrees between Uranus and the Moon, and two and five degrees between Neptune and Mars and the Moon. The seven degrees between Uranus and the Moon reinforces our Moon/Venus trine at seven degrees. Since both planets are angular and cardinal, this times our sale in seven days. The Miltons bought the house seven days later on October 25th. **NOTE:** This is the only time in Horary Astrology where you may use waning aspects — to verify time frames.

When answering timing questions (or any Horary questions) it is important to know that what is asked about is possible. Some people ask questions that are impossible to answer. I once had a couple inquire how soon some property would sell. There was no connection between the seller (1st house), the property (4th house) and the buyer (7th house). The Moon was not making an aspect to any of the rulers of these houses, so I replied that it didn't look promising in the near future. They explained that the property was not yet on the market and they weren't even sure if they wanted to sell it. When I questioned their need for the Horary, they replied that if I had said it would sell soon, they would have put out a "for sale" sign. The proper question should have been, "Should we put the house on the market?" Then the astrologer could have looked at aspects between the 1st and 4th houses for the answer. It is very important, as you can see from the above example, that the question is thought out, clearly stated and that the astrologer understands what the querent wants to know, and that the question is **answerable.**

A question that often arises with clients is how long a Horary chart is valid. Some astrologers say six weeks to three months. Frankly, it is hard to tell. If a querent wants to know if s/he will get married this year, quite possibly the chart covers that amount of time. Generally speaking, I tell clients not to ask the same question until about six weeks has elapsed. As time passes, you will become more proficient in these areas. Certainly, there are no hard and fast rules about this. Some examples of unanswerable Horary questions are: "Will I ever marry?" "When will the war end?" "When will my father die?"

More On Timing

As stated earlier, but it bears repeating, timing in the Horary chart is one of the most difficult areas to master. Of the many rules given in various Horary books, most work sometimes, but none work all the time. My experience has been that the easiest way to time the outcome of a question, presuming the question has been asked that way, is to examine the planets ruling the querent and the question and see how many degrees apart they are. Example: "How soon will I go to work on the new job?" Count how many degrees there are between the ruler of the 1st house (querent) and the ruler of the 6th (work). If there are seven degrees, then it is possible the person will go to work in seven days, weeks or months. Sounds simple, doesn't it? But wait, is it weeks, months or days?

Here are some charts to illustrate timing.

Answering Timing Questions

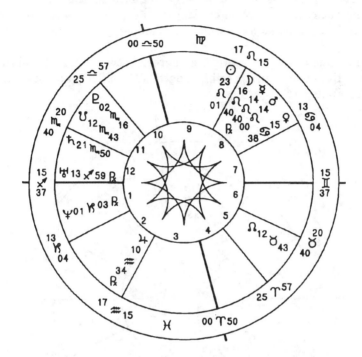

Example Chart #4:
15 Aug 1985 3:19 pm PDT Los Angeles, CA 34N01 118W15
"When will we sell the house in Topanga Canyon?"

The client who asked this question had placed her house on the market several months earlier and was becoming concerned about whether it would ever sell. Whenever you consider any kind of sale, the houses involved are the 1st and the 7th. One represents the buyer and the other the seller. Since the questioner is the seller, in this case the Ascendant signifies her. There must be an agreement between her and the buyer (7th house) for a sale to come about. (If she had been the buyer, she still would have been represented by the 1st house, because she asked the question. Remember, the querent is **always** the 1st house.)

Jupiter, ruler of the 1st, signifies her. Mercury, ruler of the 7th, shows the potential buyer. Mercury at 14 Leo had just opposed Jupiter at 10 Aquarius. Both are in Fixed signs in Succedent houses, therefore our time frame is lengthy. Months, rather than days or weeks. For confirmation of this timing, the 4th cusp at 0 Aries (indicative of the property) will trine the Moon in 16 degrees. Sixteen weeks equals approximately four months. Also in 16 degrees, Mars the significator of the property (it rules the 4th house) will quincunx the 4th house cusp.

The question was asked on August 15th, the property sold on November 15th, and escrow closed in December, just about four months later.

In timing questions count the degrees between planets relating to the question to measure possible length of time. They do not need to be making an aspect.

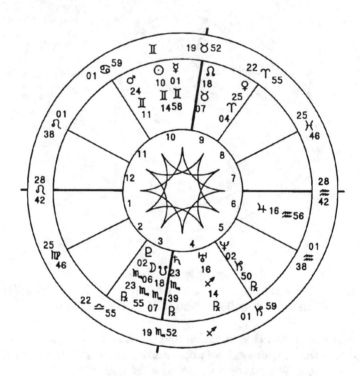

Example Chart #5:
31 May 1985 11:20 am PDT Coeur d'Alene, ID 47N41 116W46
"When will my business improve?"

This woman owned a nail salon and supply company and her business had been on a downward spiral. She wanted to know when it would improve so she would know how to handle supply orders as well as employees.

The business is represented by Venus at 25 Aries, ruler of the 10th house in the 9th. This chart validates the question, as much of her business is done by mail order to clients in distant places. Profit and loss from the business is signified by the 11th house (2nd from the 10th and therefore representative of money from the business). The ruler, the Moon at nearly 7 Scorpio, will quincunx Venus in about 18 degrees, which suggests a time frame of 18 days, weeks or months. Venus is in a Cardinal sign (Aries) and Cadent house (9th) = fast and moderately fast. The Moon is in a Fixed sign (Scorpio) and Cadent house (3rd) = slow and moderately fast. So it looks like moderately fast or in about 18 weeks. The quincunx indicates a change; Venus and the Moon are both positive factors in Horary Astrology.

Finding backup confirmation is always important. Since we are inquiring about a business, it makes sense to look at the 10th house. The MC at nearly 20 Taurus will conjunct the Sun at 10 Gemini in about 20 degrees; 20 weeks is less than five months. The Moon is 4½ degrees away from Pluto. Voila! More confirmation. In just about that time frame, she received a large out-of-state order for nail supplies and from then on, business picked up considerably.

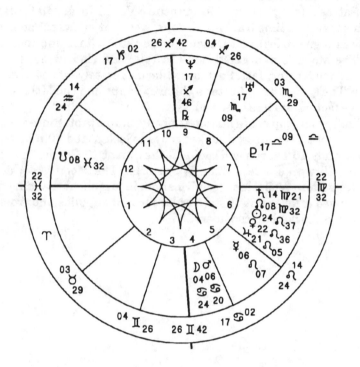

Example Chart #6:
17 Aug 1979 8:49 pm PDT Coeur d'Alene, ID 47N41 116W46
"Will we get the house in Fernan Village? When will we find out?"

Some friends had made a bid on a house nearby. They are represented by Neptune at 17 Sagittarius, ruler of the Ascendant and the house in question, the 4th, is ruled by Mercury at 6 Leo. Mercury trines Neptune, so they will definitely get the house. The Moon at 4 Cancer will conjunct Mars in the 4th house in two degrees, so we figured they would hear in two days. (Moon and Mars are both in Cardinal signs in an Angular house). She asked the question at 8:49 pm and at 10:40 pm, the realtor called and said the owner had accepted the offer. It was two hours, not two days.

When you measure time, remember it does not matter whether the planets are applying or separating. But this is the first and last time you do not adhere to the **applying only** rule.

RELATIONSHIP QUESTIONS

WILL HE MARRY ME? DOES SHE LOVE ME?
7TH HOUSE QUESTIONS

As I keep reiterating, it is most important to designate the proper houses to the components of the question. The 1st house always represents the questioner, whether singular or plural. People often ask if this rule changes when the question is "Should **we** buy the house **we** looked at today?" Whoever and how many ask the question, he, she or they are represented by the 1st house. This is an easy rule to accept after you have done a few Horary charts.

What is tricky is determining which house to assign to the person **asked about.** Many times the question will be similar to "Should I marry Bob?" In this case the person who inquired is represented by the 1st house and Bob, the second person mentioned, is signified by the 7th house. In answering a question like this, examine the aspects between the rulers of the 1st and 7th houses, any planets in them and the Moon, which co-rules the question. If the rulers of the 1st and 7th **apply** to a conjunction, trine or sextile, the answer is "yes." If, however, they **apply** to a square or opposition, the answer is "no." If it is a quincunx, something will have to change before anything will happen. Use the Moon to confirm the answer. If the Moon contradicts the planetary answer, go with the planets.

But what if there is no aspect? No aspect suggests no action, so while you do not see a "no" answer, you do not see a "yes" answer either. Again consider the lunar aspects (applying only, of course). What if the Moon does not apply to the ruler of the 7th house? Then the final thing to check are aspects to planets in either house. These aspects can be from planets in the 1st to the ruler of the 7th, planets in the 7th to the ruler of the 1st, or planets in both houses to each other. The primary rule still stands: applying aspects only. If there is no connection between the houses at all, it is unlikely there will be any connection between the people in question.

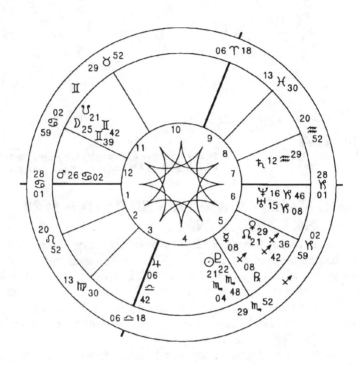

Example Chart #7:
12 Nov 1992 8:40 pm PST Coeur d'Alene, ID 47N41 116w46
"Should I stay in San Francisco and work on my relationship?"

The woman who asked the question is shown by the ruler of the Ascendant, the Moon at 25 Gemini in the 11th. Her relationship (7th house) is ruled by Saturn at 12 Aquarius in the 7th. The Moon and Saturn make no aspect. San Francisco is described by her 4th house ruled by Venus at 29 Sagittarius in the 5th. The Moon opposes Venus suggesting that she should not stay there and the lack of an aspect between the Moon and Saturn hints that the relationship doesn't have much future. She left and is happier.

But what if she had asked: "Should I leave San Francisco and end my relationship?" The astrological reasoning would be the same, but the answer would be: "No, don't leave." The Moon opposed Venus. You can see that you must be sure you understand the question and you must answer it as stated by the querent.

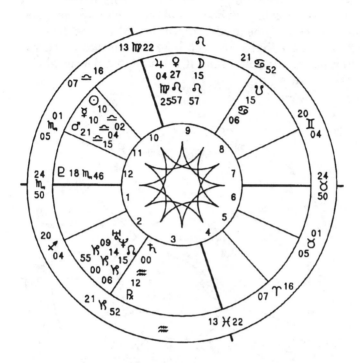

Example Chart #8:
3 Oct 1991 10:58 am PDT Coeur d'Alene, ID 47N41 116W46
"Should I use Connor as my attorney?"

The querent was having problems with tenants in some rental property and needed a good lawyer. Her question was prompted by having a list of recommended attorneys and she had decided that Connor was a likely candidate. She is represented by Mars at 21 Libra in the 11th. Remember, Mars is the main ruler of the Scorpio Ascendant; Pluto at 18 Scorpio in the 12th also signifies her as does the co-ruler Moon in the 9th of legal matters. Connor, the attorney, is designated by the 7th house ruler, Venus at 28 Leo in the 9th. The chart reflects the legal theme of the question very well. There is no applying aspect between Venus (him) and Mars (her). However, the Moon which co-rules her will conjunct Venus in the 9th house. This is a definite "yes" answer. She hired him and he is doing a good job in a long, drawn-out situation.

In the above question, the client had eliminated several of the suggested lawyers and asked if she should hire one particular one. But what if she had asked, "Should I hire Connor or Mathews?" The 7th house still represents Connor, the first lawyer inquired about, but Mathews is represented by the 9th house. Why not the 7th from the 7th? Because that is the 1st house and already represents the querent. It cannot successfully be used to represent the second attorney. This is why I keep urging that when you hear the question, you write down your approach or carefully think it through and decide where you will look for the answer.

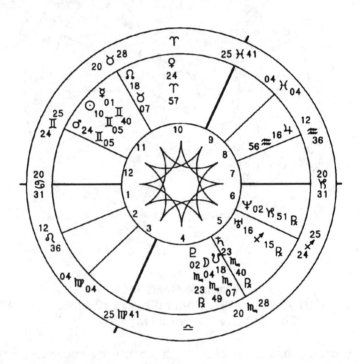

Example Chart #9:
31 May 1985 7:55 am PDT Coeur d'Alene, ID 47N41 116W46
"Should I go into business with my brother?"

Since the querent did not name his brother, I used the 3rd house to represent the person asked about. If he had said: "Should I go into business with Jim?" I would have used the 7th house to designate Jim. The Ascendant ruler representing the querent is the Moon at 4 Scorpio. His brother is described by Mercury at 1 Gemini, ruler of the 3rd house. The Moon is past an applying aspect to Mercury, indicating a lack of action between the two people. Neptune at 2 Capricorn rules the 10th house, significator of the business. The Moon is past a sextile to Neptune, and Mercury applies to a quincunx to it. This suggests that the brother might want to make changes in the business and the questioner may not want to make any changes.

This gentleman had asked a lot of Horary questions, and did not always act on my advice. He took his brother and his wife into his business and within a year, they had taken over a good share of it, moved and left him with accumulated debts, a feeling of sadness because of the breach in the family, and a healthier respect for Horary Astrology.

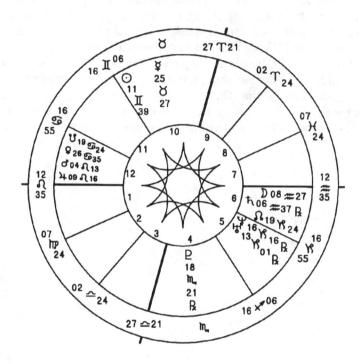

Example Chart #10:
2 June 1991 9:46 am PDT Coeur d'Alene, ID 47N41 116W46
"Is this relationship over?"

A woman who was in a serious romantic relationship asked this question. She and her boyfriend were having some problems communicating and she was in a quandary. She still loved him, but felt he was backing away from her. She is represented by the Sun in Gemini in the 10th house, as well as the Moon in Aquarius in the 6th. This validates the question quite well since they worked together. There are two ways to consider this question. Relationships are traditionally 7th house, and her question pertained to the relationship, but questions about a lover can also be assigned to the 5th house. In a situation like this, it is wise to look at both. However, this is a decision that should be made before you look at the chart. Again, remember you will get better results and find it easier to be objective, if you have outlined on paper or in your own mind the process you plan to use to answer the question.

If we place the relationship in the 7th house, Uranus at 13 Capricorn rules it and is in the 5th — a validation for using the 5th as well as the 7th. The Sun at 11 Gemini quincunxes Uranus, suggesting a change of some sort. The Moon at 8 Aquarius makes no aspect to Uranus (remember, we use major, applying aspects only: conjunction, sextile, square, trine, quincunx and opposition). Jupiter rules the 5th house; it is at 9 Leo in the 12th and the Moon opposes it. There is no aspect from the Sun to Jupiter (the sextile is past or waning). Based on these aspects I told her it looked as though it was over. She accepted the answer as likely, but pursued the affair for almost two more months — the time it took for the Sun/Uranus quincunx to become exact (in the chart, not literally). The next time I heard from her she had met someone else.

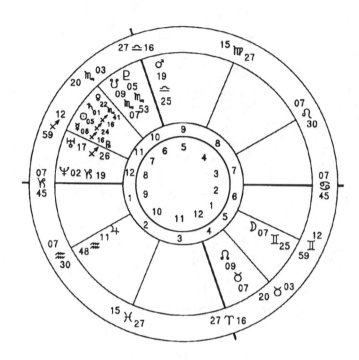

Example Chart #11:
27 Nov 1985 9:08 am PST Los Angeles, CA 34N04 118W15
"Will my son be okay if I let him go with his father?"

A client who is divorced asked this question. The father planned to take the boy on a vacation and the mother was worried that something might happen to her son.

Since she did not refer to the boy by name but as "my son," the 5th house represents the boy. In a case like this, it is wise to renumber the houses of the chart, starting with the 5th as 1, the 6th as 2 and so on. Many Horary astrologers turn the chart and put the 5th house on the Ascendant. I find it is easier to renumber. You must choose what works for you. Her son is depicted by Venus at 22 Scorpio in his 7th (11th of the chart) and co-ruler Moon at 7 Gemini which is in his 1st house (5th of the chart). His father is shown by Uranus at 17 Sagittarius, ruler of his 10th (the 2nd house in the chart) and Jupiter at 11 Aquarius which is in that house. There is no aspect between Venus and Uranus, rulers of the son's 1st and 10th, but the Moon trines Jupiter indicating that all will be well. It was.

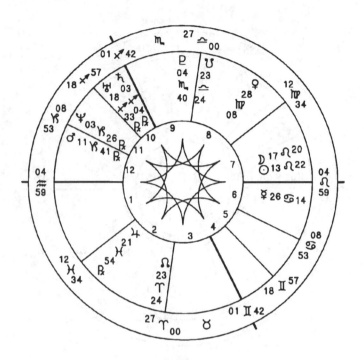

Example Chart #12:
5 Aug 1986 7:48 pm PDT Coeur d'Alene, ID 47N41 116W46
"Should Steve hire Candy?"

This example is a bit tricky. Neither Steve nor Candy asked the question. But the questioner is still the 1st house. Thus, Steve (the first person inquired about) becomes the 7th house and Candy is represented by the 1st house (Steve's 7th). This is the customary way to deal with questions about two people: use the 7th from the house asked about. In Chart #6, you will recall, I couldn't use the 7th from the 7th because it represented the querent, so I used the 2nd from the 7th to signify the second lawyer. Both the Sun at 13 Leo, ruler of Steve and the Moon at 17 Leo which is in his 1st house, apply to a trine to Uranus at 18 Sagittarius, the ruler of Candy. The answer is "yes." Steve's wife, who asked the question, reported that he had hired Candy and was very pleased with her work.

Even though it was Steve's wife who asked the question and is characterized by the 1st house, she had no bearing on the outcome of the decision so her relationship to Steve does not affect the answer.

You may be asked a question like "Will Bob leave his wife and marry me?" If the questioner is the 1st house and Bob is the 7th, where is his wife? These are difficult charts to interpret. I often place "Bob" in the 5th (since he is the querent's lover). Then his wife becomes the 11th (7th from the 5th) and depending upon the aspects among the 1st (questioner), the 5th (Bob) and the 11th (his wife), an answer may be available. In a question of this kind, the Moon is co-ruler of the querent.

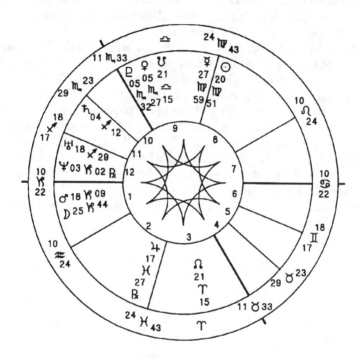

Example Chart #13:
13 Sep 1986 3:53 pm PDT Coeur d'Alene, ID 47N41 116W46
"Will my mother and brother be safe on their trip?"

The querent's relatives were planning a trip to Europe and in view of many recent highjackings, she was worried.

Her mother is represented by Venus at 5 Scorpio, ruler of the 4th house, and her brother by Neptune at 3 Capricorn, ruler of the 3rd. The mother's 9th (long trips, 12th of the chart) is ruled by Jupiter at 17 Pisces and Venus applies to a trine to Jupiter. Her brother's 9th house (11th of the chart) is ruled by Mars, Pluto (rulers) as well as Saturn which is in the house. Neptune which rules him makes no aspect to

Saturn at 4 Sagittarius or to Mars at 18 Capricorn. (Mars has passed Neptune.) It does, however, sextile Pluto at 5 Scorpio. Their journey was safe and enjoyable. If Jupiter and Venus had been square or if Mars was conjunct Neptune, I would have advised against the trip.

You may question the use of the 4th house as representing the mother. If you choose to use the 10th house for mother and the 4th house for father, that is fine. Again I remind you, the choice is yours, but it is vitally important to be consistent. I don't advise using 4th/10th for mother/father one time and 4th/10th for father/mother another. As stated before, **consistency breeds accuracy**.

When you answer questions relating to other people, keep your approach to the chart as simplistic as possible. If a person asks about a child, don't worry about which child it is. Go directly to the 5th house as a starting point, even if you know it is the querent's 3rd child. If, on the other hand someone asks "Should I send my oldest daughter and youngest son to vacation camp?" it would be important to know which child the youngest son is and look to the 5th for the older child (7th for the second child, 9th for the 3rd, etc.) and whatever house designates him. If the client had asked, "Should I give my children piano lessons?" it would be a 5th house question all the way. If you have both yes and no answers, you might suggest that the oldest child take lessons, while the youngest child does not.

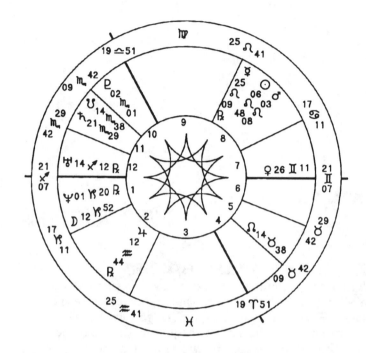

Example Chart #14:
29 July 1985 5:30 pm PDT Coeur d'Alene, ID 47N41 116W46
"Is this the right man for me?"

A lady with many romantic yearnings was longing to find the right spouse and this was the third man she had asked about in the past year.

She is ruled by Jupiter in the 2nd house at 12 Aquarius. He is represented by Mercury at 25 Leo, ruler of the 7th. Jupiter and Mercury make no aspect. Venus at 26 Gemini is in the 7th house and makes no aspect to Neptune at 1 Capricorn in the 1st or to Jupiter. Neptune makes no aspect to Jupiter. Not much going on here. The Moon at 12 Capricorn will eventually quincunx Venus in the 7th and Mercury in the 9th, but does not aspect either of her rulers. My answer was that he was not her "right man." She married him anyway and it lasted less than a year.

PURCHASES & SALES

WILL I GET MY DREAM HOUSE?

Which house represents the buyer and which signifies the seller? This is a very fine point which must be thoroughly understood by the Horary astrologer. When someone asks, "When will my house sell?" that person is represented by the 1st house (querent). In this case, the property is denoted by the 4th house and the seller is depicted by the 7th.

If the question is "Will Mr. Johnson buy my house?" the key houses are the same. The seller who is asking the question is naturally the 1st house. Mr. Johnson is the person of the 7th house. In both questions the aspects among the ruler of the 1st, the ruler of the 4th and the ruler of the 7th must be considered to obtain an answer; also the Moon and planets in the houses. If there are more favorable aspects between these planets, the answer is "yes." More unfavorable aspects, the answer is "no." In both these examples the **seller** is always the 1st house, because s/he asked the question.

"Should I buy the apartment building I looked at today?" In this instance a **buyer** is asking the question and thus becomes the 1st house. Therefore, the 7th house represents the seller and there would have to be a positive aspect between either the 1st and 7th house rulers or between the rulers of the 1st (buyer) and 4th (property). Let's use a hypothetical chart to answer this question. Mars rules the 1st house and Venus the 7th and there is **no** applying aspect between them. The Moon, which is always the co-ruler of the chart, rules the 4th house of property and is applying to a trine of Mars. This would indicate that the property is a good buy and the questioner should consider it. But what about no action with the seller? Check if there are other planets in the 1st or

7th houses and the aspects they make to each other or the rulers. If there is any kind of major aspect linking the buyer and the seller, there is the opportunity to make some kind of deal. Certainly an offer is appropriate.

One more factor in making a decision whether a sale or purchase will come about is the exchange of money. If you have an article for sale and there is an aspect between the buyer's money house (the 8th) and your 1st house, this can be an indication that the sale will take place if the aspect is a trine or sextile, that there must be a price adjustment if the two planets make a quincunx, that the sale will not occur if the aspect is a square or opposition. Obviously, if the planets make no aspect, nothing much will happen.

Real estate purchases are pretty cut and dried, but what about other kinds of buying and selling? There are two schools of thought about this. Some astrologers feel you should use the house that describes the item, *i.e.,* gold — 5th house, books — 3rd, office equipment — 6th or 10th and so on. After interpreting many of these charts, I find it gives better results to use the house of possessions (the 2nd) to represent whatever you wish to purchase.

The chart will usually reflect the item of concern. For instance, if you're questioning the purchase of a sewing machine, rulers of the 2nd and Ascendant or the Moon may fall into the 3rd house which has to do with sewing machines. If you ask, "Should I buy a new filing cabinet for my office?" often significators will appear in the 6th or 10th houses.

It is much easier to ask a purchase question about a single item, but you can ask questions like, "Should I buy the Singer sewing machine? If not, should I buy the Bernina?" To answer this question, you would consider aspects between the 1st house ruler (querent) and the ruler of the 2nd house in regard to the Singer. If they are positive, you need go no further. If they are negative then consider aspects between the rulers of the 1st and 3rd houses. The 3rd is the 2nd from the 2nd and signifies the second item asked about.

In dealing with property, someone may ask you whether to buy the house on 3rd Street or the one by the golf course. The 3rd Street house is represented by the 4th house and the house near the golf course is denoted by the 7th house (4th from the 4th). The following examples will help to clarify this approach.

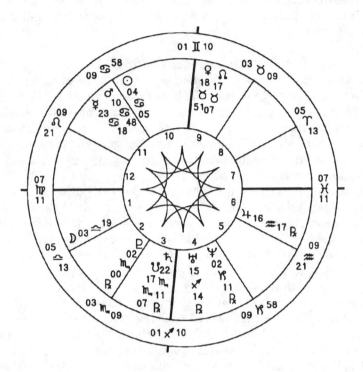

Example Chart #15:
25 Jun 1985 10:28 am PDT Coeur d'Alene, ID 47N41 116W46
"Should we buy a new trailer hitch?"

The querent is represented by Mercury at 23 Cancer in the 11th house and the Moon at 3 Libra in the 1st. The trailer hitch is denoted by Venus at 18 Taurus, ruler of the 2nd in the 9th. Mercury makes no aspect to Venus and the Moon quincunxes it. The lack of aspect shows little action and the quincunx suggests that some intervening event may occur. Shortly after he asked this question, the gentleman sold the trailer and had no need for a new hitch.

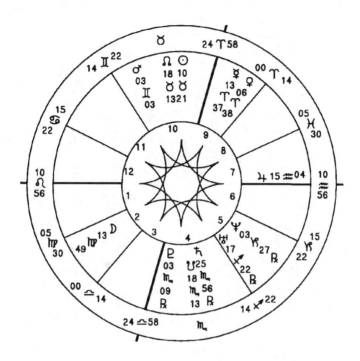

Example Chart #16:
30 Apr 1985 11:45 am PDT Coeur d'Alene, ID 47N41 116W46
"Will the Harrisons buy the house for $205,000?"

The querent is the 1st house ruled by the Sun at 10 Taurus in the 10th. The potential buyer is represented by the ruler of the 7th house, Uranus at 17 Sagittarius in the 5th. The Sun quincunxes Uranus indicating adjustments to be made before a sale of property will take place. The Moon, which is always the co-ruler of the chart, is at 13 Virgo in the 2nd and squares Uranus representing the potential buyer, suggesting the price is too high. The people were very interested; Venus at 6 Aries rules the 4th (the property) and trines Uranus which rules them and also sextiles Jupiter at 15 Aquarius in the 7th. The woman who asked the question was advised to lower the price and negotiate terms. After much haggling the buyer and seller agreed on a lower price and better interest arrangements and the house was sold.

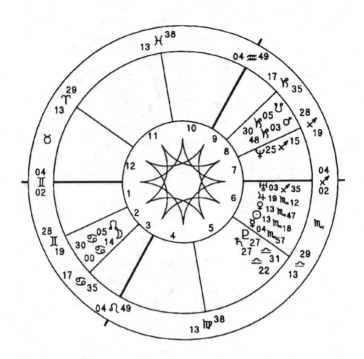

Example Chart #17:
5 Nov 1982 5:16 pm PST Coeur d'Alene, ID 47n41 116w46
"Is Mr. Moore going to buy the business Monday?"

A client's husband had died and she was trying to dispose of his large trucking business. She had many prospects and Mr. Moore was going to make an offer on the following Monday.

The buyer is indicated by Jupiter, ruler of the 7th, at 19 Scorpio in the 6th. Mercury, ruler of the 1st, is also in the 6th at 4 Scorpio and will conjunct Jupiter in 15 degrees, suggesting a possible "yes" answer, but certainly not on Monday, which was only 3 days away. The question was about a business, so the 10th house must also be taken into consideration. Uranus at 3 Sagittarius rules the 10th and receives no aspect from Jupiter representing the buyer; so even though there was a connection between buyer and seller, there was no connection between the buyer and the business. The Moon at 14 Cancer trines Jupiter signifying the potential buyer and also his money (rules the 8th), but in spite of this, the answer looked like no. He might offer, but she wouldn't accept. The potential buyer did not purchase the business on Monday. However, he made a low offer 15 days later, just about when Mercury conjuncted Jupiter. It was rejected.

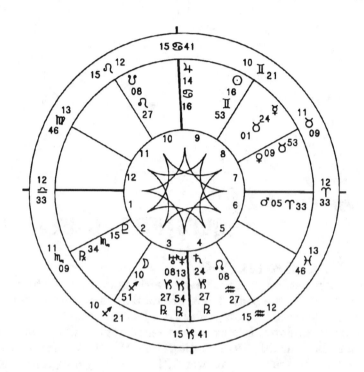

Example Chart #18:
7 Jun 1990 2:51 pm PDT Coeur d'Alene, ID 47N41 116W46
"Should I buy the tractor I looked at today?"

The client had been looking for a tractor for his growing gardening business and was having difficulty making up his mind about which of the many he had seen was the one to buy. His wife suggested that he call and ask a Horary question.

He is Venus at 9 Taurus in the 7th and the tractor is Mars, ruler of the 2nd, at 5 Aries in the 6th. A very valid chart, since the tractor is machinery and Mars rules machines. However, there is no aspect between Mars and Venus. Pluto co-rules the tractor and is in the 2nd house at 15 Scorpio. Venus opposes it. The Moon should be taken into consideration. It is at 10 Sagittarius, past both the trine to Mars and the quincunx to Venus. I told the man that this wasn't the tractor for him that he should look further. A few weeks later he called and asked the same question about a different tractor. This time the answer was a clear "yes" and he was very satisfied with his purchase.

LESSON VIII
QUESTIONS ABOUT HEALTH

OH, MY ACHING BACK!

Every Horary astrologer must have a working concept of which planet rules each part of the body. There are numerous astrology books that address this subject. *The Only Way To... Learn Astrology — Vol. I* also gives a brief rundown. Basic common sense applies when you answer questions about health. **Do not diagnose.** If a client asks a question that you feel you are able to answer without offering diagnostic suggestions, that is fine. Unless you have medical training, and even if you do, be careful in this area.

When replying to queries about health, you must consider the 1st (physical body) as well as the 6th house, and often these questions are better judged by a careful perusal of the natal chart, presuming that one is available.

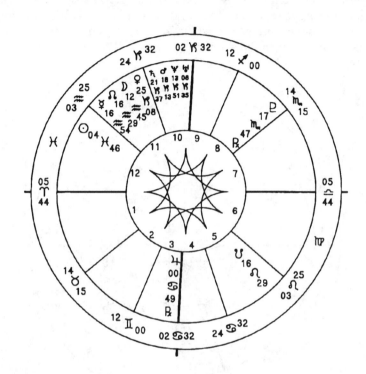

Example Chart #19:
23 Feb 1990 7:45 am PST Coeur d'Alene, ID 47N41 116W46
"Should I go to the doctor about my knee?"

A client called quite early one morning, explained that her knee had been paining her for several days and her husband was nagging her to go to the doctor to see what was wrong.

She is depicted by Mars at 18 Capricorn (the sign of the knees) in the 10th house. The doctor is the 7th house, ruled by Venus at 25 Capricorn in the 11th. Venus is past the conjunction to Mars. The Sun, ruler of the 6th, at 4 Pisces applies to a 14-degree sextile to Mars, so although I felt she should go have the knee examined, the Moon made no contact to Mars, Venus or the Sun. It did, however, conjunct Mercury, ruler of the interception in the 6th house, in four degrees. I told her that if her knee was still bothering her in four days she should make an appointment. The long applying Sun/Mars sextile did not indicate immediate action. In the meantime she decided to take hot baths and see if they would help. Within a few days her knee felt fine and she never did go to the doctor.

There will be many times when common sense dictates an answer that does not appear in the chart and this presents a dilemma for the Horary astrologer. But you must have faith in your craft. Sometimes the answer may not make sense to you but will to the querent.

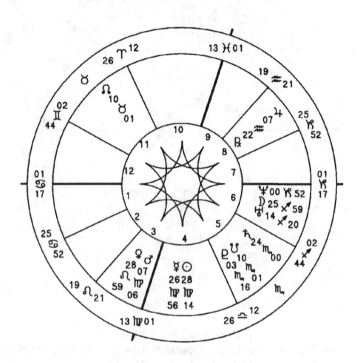

Example Chart #20:
20 Sep 1985 11:50 pm PDT Los Angeles, CA 34N04 118W15
"Will the biopsy find cancer?"

A client had discovered a lump and was scheduled for a biopsy in two days. Since she is ruled by the Moon at 26 Sagittarius in the 6th house, it was a very legitimate question. The ruler of the 6th house is Jupiter (significator of growths) at 7 Aquarius in the 8th (of surgery). The Moon made no aspect to Jupiter but squared both Mercury and the Sun. Mercury rules the 12th of hospitalization, so it looks like a "no" answer. The doctor (7th house) is ruled by Saturn which is squared by Jupiter, another "no" indicator. The lump was benign. Remember that squares and oppositions say "no," and trines and sextiles say "yes."

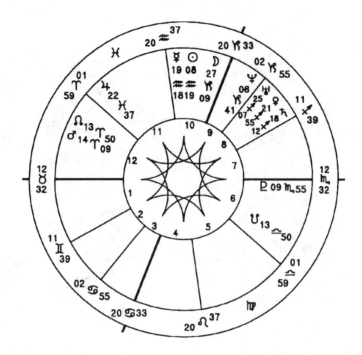

Example Chart #21:
28 Jan 1987 10:46 am PST Coeur d'Alene, ID 47N41 116W46
"Am I allergic to the shampoo I am using?"

A student asked this question because she was trying to find out what was causing an annoying rash around her hairline. Venus at nearly 22 Sagittarius rules the Ascendant as well as the 6th house and Pluto is in the 6th at almost 10 Scorpio. There is no aspect between Pluto and Venus and the Moon is void of course, all indicating a "no" answer. Venus had conjuncted Saturn a few days previously and the allergy had seemed to ease at that time. A week later the rash had totally disappeared. She never found out what had caused it.

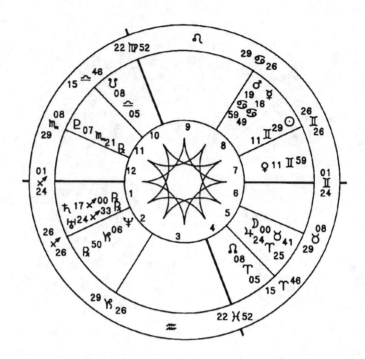

Example Chart #22:
20 Jun 1987 6:26 pm PDT Coeur d'Alene, ID 47N41 116W46
"Should I have a breast implant?"

In view of what has come to light in the news lately about silicone breast implants, this is an interesting chart. A client who had several facelifts was considering changing her bustline.

She is signified by Jupiter at 24 Aries in the 5th house; operations are the province of the 8th house. Mercury at 16 Cancer rules it and is there along with the Sun at 29 Gemini and Mars at 20 Cancer. Both Mercury and Mars (the cutting planet) square Jupiter, suggesting a "no" answer. Saturn rising confirms that conclusion. I advised her not to have the operation.

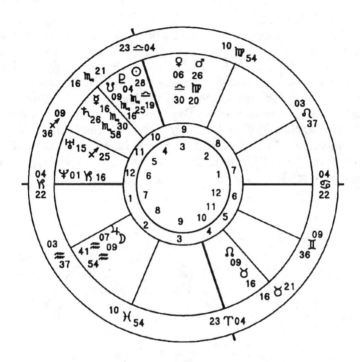

Example Chart #23:
21 Oct 1985 11:53 am MST Phoenix, AZ 33N27 112W04
"Will Mac ever walk again?"

In this chart the houses must be renumbered. The 7th represents Mac (remember, always place the named person in the 7th house); therefore his 6th house is the 12th of the chart. Mac is designated by the Moon at 9 Aquarius in his 8th. The ruler of his 6th is Jupiter at 7 Aquarius also in his 8th, but the Moon is past the conjunction to Jupiter. This doesn't look favorable. Mars has to do with action and locomotion so since the question is about "walking," it is necessary to consider Mars in assessing the answer to this question. It is at 26 Virgo in Mac's 3rd house. Mercury rules the 3rd house and at 16 Scorpio sextiles Mars, but it is a ten-degree aspect. The Moon quincunxes Mars and squares Mercury; since the Moon is in his 8th, it looks as though surgery may not help. Mac had been injured in an auto accident and was paralyzed from the waist down. His mother had asked the question. When given the answer, she replied that the doctors had recommended a surgeon who offered a slight bit of hope that an operation may be successful, but it was a long shot. The last I heard he never had the operation and was still confined to a wheel chair.

Other 6th House Questions

ALL IN A DAY'S WORK

Jobs and job-related questions are also 6th house concerns. Let me note here that if someone asks about taking or getting a job, the question is properly placed in the 6th house. If the person has a current job (6th house) but asks about another job, place that question in the 11th house (the 6th from the 6th). Some Horary astrologers use the 10th house to indicate job. I prefer to reserve the 10th for questions pertaining to career and vocational fields. You may wish to try the 10th house for job-related questions. Then a second job would be represented by the 7th, the 10th from the 10th. Again, decide beforehand which approach you will use, then stick to your chosen path.

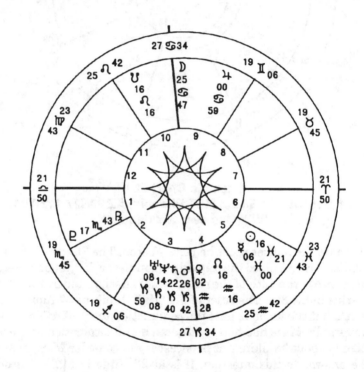

Example Chart #24:
6 Mar 1990 8:47 pm PST Coeur d'Alene, ID 47N41 116W46
"Should I take the job at Shenanigan's (a restaurant)?"

A student was trying to decide whether to take a part time job while she finished her last year in school.

She is Venus in the 4th house at 2 Aquarius; the job is Neptune at 14 Capricorn, ruler of the 6th in the 3rd. There is no aspect between these planets. The Moon's only aspect at 25 Cancer is an opposition to Mars in the 3rd. The answer was "no," don't take the job. With the very active 3rd house it looked like she needed all her time to study.

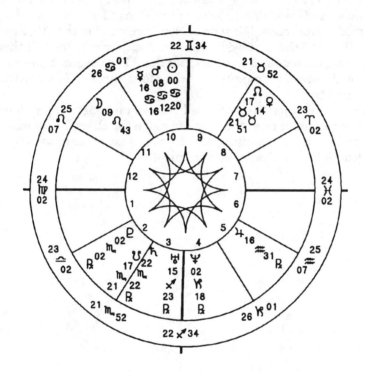

Example Chart #25:
21 Jun 1985 12:15 pm PDT Coeur d'Alene, ID 47N41 116W46
"Should I quit my current job and go into business with Miranda?"

The girl who asked the question was working as a waitress in a very busy local restaurant. A friend was opening a new restaurant down the street and wanted the querent to go in with her in the new business.

The questioner is Mercury at 16 Cancer in the 10th house; her current job is signified by Uranus ruling the 6th at 15 Sagittarius in the 3rd. The business (10th) is also ruled by Mercury, but Mars and the Sun are also in this house. Mercury and Uranus make no (applying) aspect to each other and Mercury is past both Mars and the Sun. Not much in the way of an answer. Miranda (depicted by the 7th house) is represented by Neptune at 2 Capricorn and Mercury makes no aspect to Neptune. The last thing we consider is the Moon. It is at 9 Leo in the 11th house and trines Uranus, ruler of her current job. It was suggested that she stay where she was, since it didn't look like Miranda would get the business off the ground. She stayed with the job; the restaurant never opened.

I used this chart in class and a student asked why I hadn't used the 4th house for Miranda's business. I replied that I didn't think of it, but let's try that approach. Miranda is Neptune, ruler of the 7th; her 10th is the 4th of the chart, ruled by Jupiter. Neptune is in the 4th showing her interest in opening a business, but there is no aspect between Neptune and Jupiter 16 Aquarius and the Moon opposes Jupiter. The answer is still "no."

It is always wise to exercise all options in doing Horary charts. If there is a second or even third way to judge the chart, by all means do it. Invariably it will confirm your answer. Just as in natal astrology, you need all the confirmation you can get.

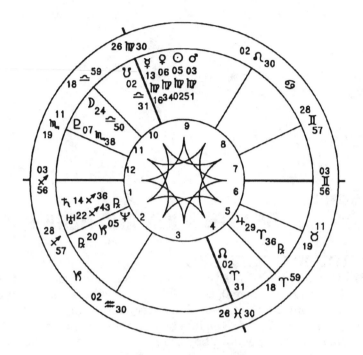

Example Chart #26:
28 Aug 1987 2:08 pm PDT Coeur d'Alene, ID 47N41 116W46
"Will I get the job in Washington, D.C.?"

A professor at Washington State University applied for a position as Executive Director of a professional organization in Washington, D.C., and called to see if she would be selected for the position.

Jupiter at 29 Aries rules the Ascendant and designates her. Saturn and Uranus at 14 and 22 Sagittarius respectively in the 1st house are also her significators. The new job is the 11th house (6th from the 6th) and is ruled by Venus at 6 Virgo. The Moon and Pluto are also there, suggesting that this is a valid question. Venus' placement in the 9th also validates the question; Washington, D.C., is a long distance away. Jupiter the Ascendant ruler is quincunxed by Venus, ruler of the 6th. Venus squares Saturn and Uranus in the 1st. Things don't look too promising. The Moon, which co-rules her, is at 24 Libra in the 11th and opposes Jupiter, her primary ruler. Neither the Moon nor Pluto makes any aspects to Saturn or Uranus in the 1st, and Saturn rising confirms the "no" answer given by the other positions. She was not selected for the job.

LESSON IX
OF KITH & KIN AND HERE & NOW

3RD HOUSE QUESTIONS

The 3rd house answers questions about the local environment, short trips (both time and mileage), cars, siblings, neighbors, tests (examinations) of any kind, contracts and elementary education.

Questions like: "Should I go into business with my brother?" "Will I pass my math test?" "Should I buy the Honda Accord?" "Should I go to Seattle for the weekend (if you live close by)?"

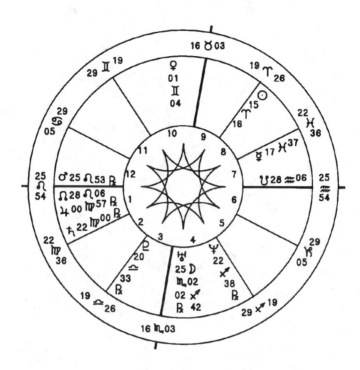

Example Chart #27:
4 Apr 1980 1:48 pm PST Coeur d'Alene, ID 47N41 116W46
"Will I pass the real estate test tomorrow?"

The Sun at 15 Aries rules the querent (1st house) and is in the 8th house. Tests of any kind are a 3rd house question. The 3rd house ruler, Venus at 1 Gemini, is in the 10th and will eventually sextile the Sun. That's a "yes." The Moon which is always the co-ruler of the question is at 2 Sagittarius, just past the opposition to Venus, but applying to a trine to the Sun, indicating another "yes." The Sun opposes Pluto in the 3rd house at 20 Libra which is a "no." Jupiter rising confirms a "yes" answer. With three yesses and one no, I told the client she would pass the test, but it wouldn't hurt to study a lot between now and when she took it (Sun opposition Pluto). She did and passed with a respectable grade.

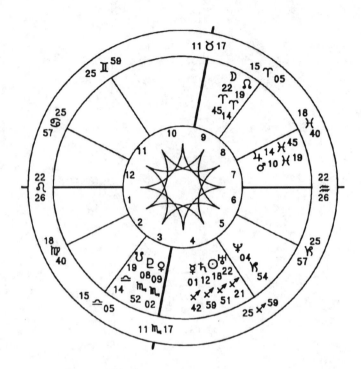

Example Chart #28:
10 Dec 1986 9:04 pm PST Coeur d'Alene, ID 47N41 116W46
"Did a neighbor steal my money?"

A young man who operated a business in his home was missing a large amount of money. He asked earlier who had stolen the money and the description seemed to fit a neighbor, hence, this second question. The neighbor is ruled by Venus (ruler of the 3rd in the 3rd house) at 9 Scorpio; the man's money is signified by Mercury at 1 Sagittarius (2nd house). There is no aspect between Mercury and Venus and the Moon at 22 Aries does not aspect either one. The answer is "no." It was later determined that the money was taken by an employee.

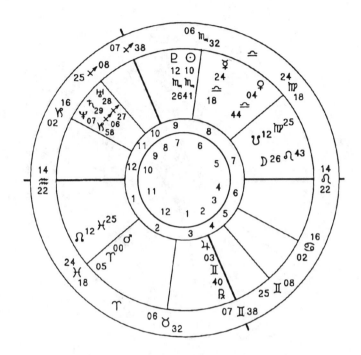

Example Chart #29:
2 Nov 1988 1:21 pm Coeur d'Alene, ID 47N41 116W46
"Will the school levy pass?"

This was a major issue in a local election and one of the candidates for mayor called and asked the question. Venus at 4 Libra (in the 8th) rules the 3rd house, representative of schools. Money from other people is an 8th house venue; it is ruled by Jupiter (the 10th house in the chart is the 8th from the 3rd). Jupiter is at 3 Gemini in the 3rd but makes no aspect to Venus. It is past the trine. The Moon at 26 Leo makes no aspect to Venus or Jupiter. Though it was very close it did not pass.

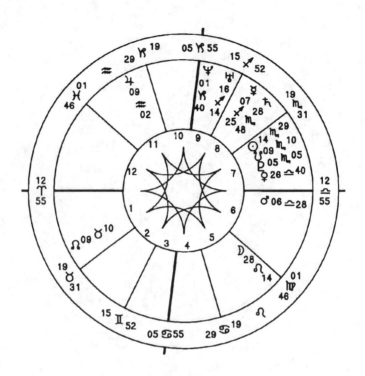

Example Chart #30:
6 Nov 1985 3:10 pm PST Pullman, WA 46N44 117W10
"Is November 22nd a good day to defend my dissertation?"

A college professor asked this question. Since a dissertation is in the nature of a test, the 3rd house should give the answer. The querent is represented by Mars at 6 Libra in the 6th; the ruler of the 3rd (the dissertation) is Mercury at 7 Sagittarius in the 8th. Mercury has just passed a sextile to Mars (one degree). It seemed she should do this about a week earlier. When we checked the ephemeris, Mercury would turn retrograde on November 19th which is not the greatest time to tackle anything involving communication. She requested to defend her dissertation a week earlier; it was approved; she got her Ph.D. In this case it is not necessary to look at the Moon which is exactly square Saturn. The planets have provided the answer. The lunar aspect confirms that November 22nd is **not** the day to defend her dissertation.

LESSON X

FLY ME TO THE MOON

9TH HOUSE QUESTIONS

Ninth house questions pertain to long-distance travel, higher education, in-laws, grandchildren and legal matters.

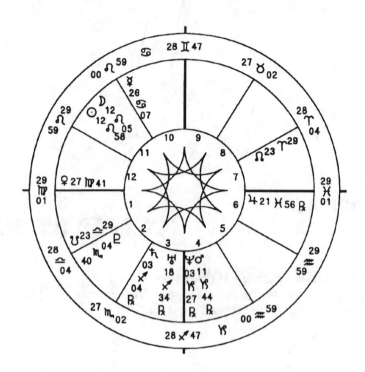

Example Chart #31:
5 Aug 1986 9:46 am PDT Coeur d'Alene, ID 47N41 116W46
"Should I go on Queen Elizabeth cruise?
Can I afford it? Will I have fun?"

This question came from a young lady. I felt she had already made up her mind since 29 degrees was rising. Remember, often late degrees rising mean the answer has already been decided or the question is moot, but I still reply to such questions. Mercury at 26 Cancer rules her (1st) and Venus at 27 Virgo rules the voyage (9th). Mercury will sextile Venus. Since Venus also rules her 2nd, it looked like she would be able to afford it. With Mercury in the 10th and the Moon at 12 Leo trine Uranus at 18 Sagittarius, ruler of the 5th of fun and games, I told her she would probably have fun and enjoy the social activities. She replied that she had already bought her ticket, but wanted to know what would happen. She took the cruise and had a marvelous time. Even though the Moon conjuncted the Sun, a major aspect in natal astrology, here since the Sun has no bearing on the question, this aspect is insignificant.

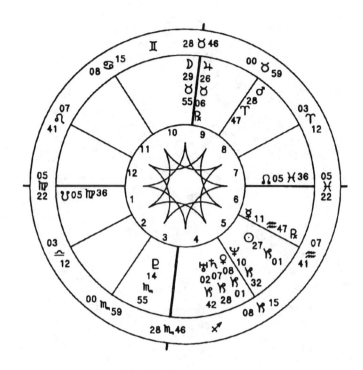

Example Chart #32:
16 Jan 1989 7:47 pm PST Coeur d'Alene, ID 47N41 116W46
"Will the court award supervised visits
from my ex-husband to my daughter?"

After a particularly messy divorce the client didn't trust her ex not to kidnap the child when he took her for visitation.

She is Mercury at 11 Aquarius in the 6th (the house of the child's future); her ex-husband is Neptune, ruler of the 7th, at 10 Capricorn in the 5th...a very valid chart. (NOTE: Just as the 12th or preceding house represents the past, so the 2nd or ensuing house describes the future.) The court (9th) is represented by Venus at 8 Capricorn applying to a conjunction of Neptune, suggesting that the court would act in some way regarding the husband. This is an example of a VOC Moon helping to answer the question. The Moon is in the 10th house in a finishing degree at 29 Taurus. Because of the void Moon and the Venus/Neptune aspect I felt she had nothing to worry about. The court ruled that supervision was necessary for his visits. She already had custody.

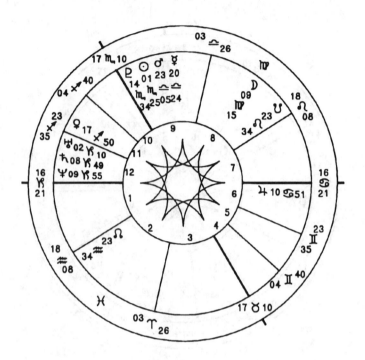

Example Chart #33:
24 Oct 1989 1:33 pm PDT Coeur d'Alene, ID 47N41 116W46
"How will everything turn out in court tomorrow
with house in Montana?"

A student called and asked this question. They owned a summer home in Montana and the people they had bought it from were suing over an alleged oversight in the mortgage. The suit required that they appear in court the next day and she was concerned about the outcome.

Saturn rules the querent and is at 8 Capricorn in the 12th showing her concern. The Moon rules the opponent (7th) and Venus rules the court. The Moon at 9 Virgo squares Venus at 17 Sagittarius, suggesting that her opponent will not fare well. The Moon is just past the trine to Saturn. I told my student that it looked like a tempest in a teapot and that they would come out all right. The judge threw the case out of court which surprised me as I hadn't anticipated that outcome. Looking at the chart in retrospect, Mars rules the judge (10th) and it is void of course, so in essence, there really was nothing to worry about.

LESSON XI

AM I HAVING FUN YET?

5TH HOUSE QUESTIONS

Fifth house questions pertain to gambling, investing, pregnancy, children or taking chances. If someone asks about a child, but does not designate the child by name, it is wise to use the 5th house as the 1st and either turn the chart to put the 5th on the Ascendant, or renumber the houses with the 5th as the 1st and so on. For instance, if the question is "Should my child go to summer camp this year?" this is answered by examining the 5th and the 9th (5th from the 5th), assuming camp is a "fun" place to go.

Any questions about games, romance, purchase of stocks, bonds or commodities and contests relate to this house, its ruler and any planets in it.

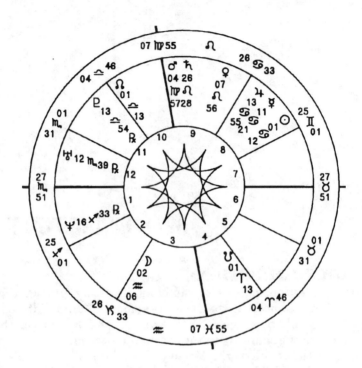

Example Chart #34:
22 Jun 1978 5:28 pm PDT Los Angeles, CA 34N04 118W15
"Are we going to win Saturday?"

This question was asked by a girls' softball coach whose team was play-ing in a championship game on Saturday and she wanted to know if they had a chance to win.

Aries is on the 5th house cusp; the ruler Mars at 4 Virgo is conjunct the Midheaven of honor and achievement and also co-rules the Scorpio Ascendant which describes the coach and her team. Mars elevated and conjunct the Midheaven is a "yes." Pluto at 13 Libra co-rules the Ascen-dant and is trined by the 2 Aquarius Moon which is the co-ruler of the question... another "yes."

Venus at nearly 8 Leo rules the opponents (7th house) and is op-posed by the Moon. Venus also rules the 11th which represents the game for the opponents. Venus is intercepted and will eventually con-junct Saturn of denial. I told the coach her team would win. They won a close game in the last inning.

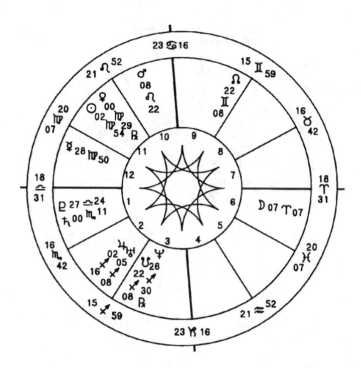

Example Chart #35:
26 Aug 1983 10:10 am PDT Coeur d'Alene, ID 47N41 116W46
"Should we buy Gold Cache stock?"

This is a question that every Horary astrologer will eventually hear. This query was presented by the president of a small corporation which was looking for a profitable investment. Venus rules the querent and is retrograde at 0 Virgo in the 11th house. Although it is conjunct the Sun, which suggests a "yes" answer, it also squares Uranus at 5 Sagittarius, ruler of the 5th house of stock purchases. Venus also squares Jupiter at 2 Sagittarius in the 2nd house of potential profit for the questioner. So far we have one "yes" and two "nos."

The Moon at 7 Aries is past any aspect to Venus or Uranus, suggesting that it is too late to profit from this investment. Saturn in the 1st house confirms the "no" answer. The gentleman called several weeks later to let me know that they hadn't purchased the stock and were very happy that they had asked the Horary question, since the stock had plummeted in value.

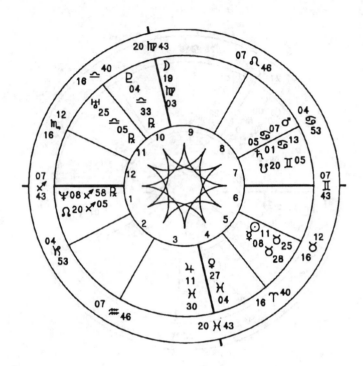

Example Chart #36:
1 May 1974 9:40 pm PDT Los Angeles, CA 34N04 118W15
"Am I pregnant? If so, will I have an abortion?"

A client called and asked this question. Her doctor had given her a test and assured her she was not pregnant, but she felt uneasy about the situation.

She is denoted by Jupiter at 11 Pisces, ruler of the Ascendant; Mars at 7 Cancer rules the 5th house and trines Jupiter. It also sextiles the Sun and Mercury at 8 and 11 Taurus in the 5th house. I told her the chart said she was pregnant. Since the Moon rules the 8th house of surgery and at 19 Virgo opposes Venus, ruler of her 6th at 27 Pisces, I wasn't sure if she would have an abortion. Mars, planet of surgery, in the 8th quincunxes the Ascendant and Neptune at 7 and 8 Sagittarius in the 1st, so it looks as though some changes would take place. Mars also trines her ruler, Jupiter. All told there were more "yes" than "no" answers. She went back to the doctor for another test which was positive. She had the abortion a week later.

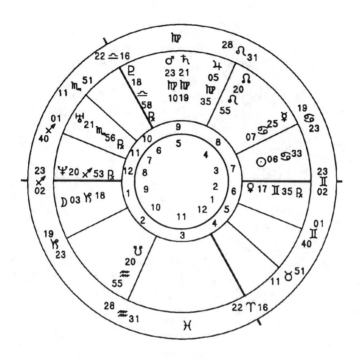

Example Chart #37:
27 Jun 1980 7:44 pm PDT Coeur d'Alene, ID 47N41 116W46
"Did my son start the fire?"

A client's young son had been accused of starting a fire that gutted a neighbor's garage. Her son denied the accusation, but she wasn't sure if he was telling the truth and thought a Horary chart might provide the answer.

Venus at 17 Gemini rules her son (5th); Saturn at 21 Virgo rules his 10th house (2nd of the chart). Venus squares Saturn, the planet of responsibility, and Mars at 23 Virgo, ruler of fire suggesting that he did **not** set the fire. (Remember squares and oppositions are "no" answers.) Here is a case where I used the 10th house to signify an event, the fire. The Moon, co-ruler of the question, at 3 Capricorn widely quincunxes Venus and trines Saturn as well as Mars. These trines might suggest a "yes" answer, but my experience has been that the planetary aspects outweigh those of the Moon, unless the Moon rules one of the houses pertaining to the question. So the answer here was "no." It was later proven that another youngster was the culprit.

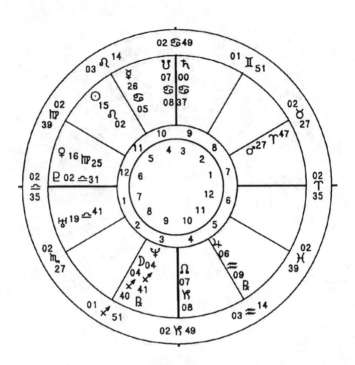

Example Chart #38:
7 Aug 1973 10:01 am PDT Los Angeles, CA 34N04 118W15
"Will Tim get custody of his kids?"

This question was asked by a friend of Tim's. Tim is represented by the 7th house, so you must either turn the chart or renumber the houses. His children are signified by his 5th, the 11th in the chart. Mars at 27 Aries rules him and the Sun at 15 Leo designates his children. The Sun trines Mars indicating a "yes." Jupiter at 6 Aquarius rules his 9th of legal matters, in this case, representing legal custody. The Moon at 4 Sagittarius is in his 9th and sextiles Jupiter and trines both the Sun and Mars confirming a "yes" answer. He went to court three weeks later and got custody of all three children.

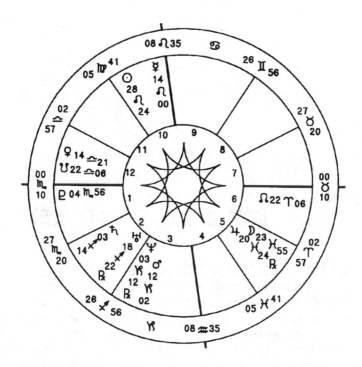

Example Chart #39:
21 Aug 1986 11:32 am PDT Coeur d'Alene, ID 47N41 116W46
"Will my daughter have her baby while I am on vacation?"

The querent's daughter was due to have her baby around the middle of September. Her vacation was to start September 1st and she didn't want to be away when her grandchild was born.

Neptune at 3 Capricorn rules the 5th (her daughter) and Mercury at 14 Leo rules the 9th (the anticipated grandchild... 5th from the 5th). There is no aspect between Mercury and Neptune so it seemed unlikely that the birth would take place sooner than expected. The Moon in the 5th house at 24 Pisces is VOC, again an indication that there was nothing to worry about. She went on the trip and her daughter delivered a week after she returned. Neptune sextiled Pluto, co-ruler of the querent, in one degree, in this case, indicating one week.

WHOSE MONEY IS IT, ANYWAY?

2ND & 8TH HOUSE QUESTIONS

Both the 2nd and 8th houses pertain to finances, and questions concerning spending, earning and all financial situations are properly placed in one of these houses. The 8th also covers sexual questions, those pertaining to affairs (along with the 5th), taxes and deaths. If someone asks about whether a romantic affair will turn into a sexual one, both the 5th and 8th houses will need examination. If someone asks about the potential for a tax audit, or recovering money loaned, the 8th comes into play.

Aside from money matters, the 2nd house is very significant in questions about lost objects. In fact, finding misplaced belongings always starts here. More about finding things in Lesson XIII. The following questions are mostly financial in nature.

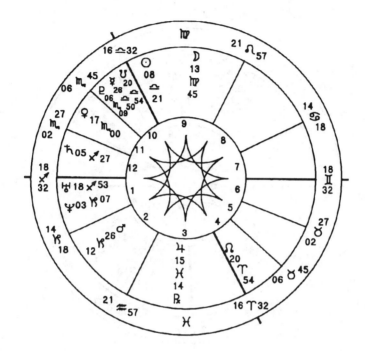

Example Chart #40:
1 Oct 1986 1:07 pm PDT Coeur d'Alene, ID 47N41 116W46
"How long should I wait to implement the loan?"

This client had applied for a home equity loan and was watching for the interest rate to go as low as possible before closing the loan papers. The rates had been dropping steadily and he was afraid to wait too long, in case they started to rise.

He is represented by Jupiter, ruler of the Ascendant, at 15 Pisces in the 3rd house of contracts. Again the chart reflects the question. Money from a lending institution is an 8th house proposition and the 8th is ruled by the Moon. The Moon is in the 9th at 13 Virgo and will oppose Jupiter in 1½ degrees. Even though the opposition is considered negative, he did not ask if he should implement the loan, only when. This aspect suggested a time frame of 1½ days or weeks since both Jupiter and the Moon are in Mutable signs and Cadent houses. Remember Cardinal/Angular is fastest, Mutable/Cadent is moderately fast and Fixed/Succedent is slow. I explained that the timing could be one and a half days or weeks.

He called the bank and decided to make an appointment to close the escrow a week and a half later and secured the loan.

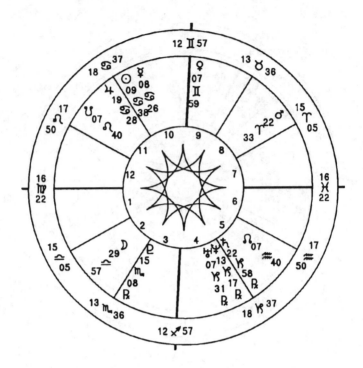

Example Chart #41:
1 Jul 1990 10:55 am PDT Coeur d'Alene, ID 47N41 116W46
"Should I borrow money to buy more cows,
rent pasture and expand my operation?"

A South Dakota rancher called and asked this question. He had a large spread and raised beef cows, but was thinking of expanding if the timing was right. Mercury at 8 Cancer rules him and is in the business 10th. Borrowing has to do with the 8th house and the ruler is Mars at 22 Aries in the 8th. Mercury squares Mars indicating a "no" answer. The Moon that co-rules the chart is in his 2nd house at 29 Libra 57 and VOC (void of course) suggesting that it will not be a money-making venture and that nothing much would come of it. The next time I heard from him he told me that he was glad he had not made the investment since the bottom dropped out of the beef market shortly afterward.

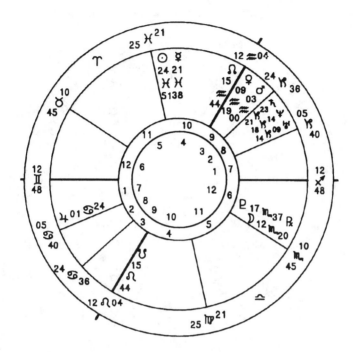

Example Chart #42:
15 Mar 1990 9:13 am PST Coeur d'Alene, ID 47N41 116W46
"Should my husband accept the settlement
from the insurance company?

The first thing to do is renumber the houses, making the 7th (husband) the 1st, the 8th the 2nd and so on around the chart; or you can turn the chart so the 7th is on the Ascendant.

Now Jupiter at 1 Cancer represents the husband and the money from the insurance company is signified by the Moon, ruler of his 8th house (2nd). At 12 Scorpio, the Moon is past the trine to Jupiter. There are no planets in his 1st or 8th houses, so without an aspect between the rulers, no answer is found and suggests no action at this time. However, the Sun at 25 Pisces rules the insurance company (10th house) and the Moon trines it. So I told the wife that her husband should decline the offer and ask for more money because it looked like the insurance company would give more. They did.

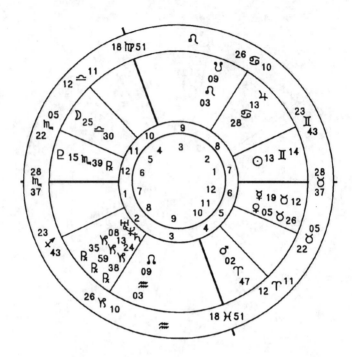

Example Chart #43:
3 Jun 1990 7:17 pm PDT Coeur d'Alene, ID 47N41 116W46
"Will Tim get the loan to buy the house on 2nd Street?"

Again the chart must be renumbered or turned. Tim becomes the 7th house and is ruled by Venus at 5 Taurus in his 12th. Money for a loan is signified by his 8th (2nd of the chart) ruled by Jupiter at 13 Cancer. Venus applies to a sextile of Jupiter, a "yes" answer. The Moon at 25 Libra is VOC... nothing to worry about. Tim's mother, who had asked the question, was very relieved as he just barely qualified and the bank seemed to be holding back. The money came through, he moved in, and hopefully is living happily ever after.

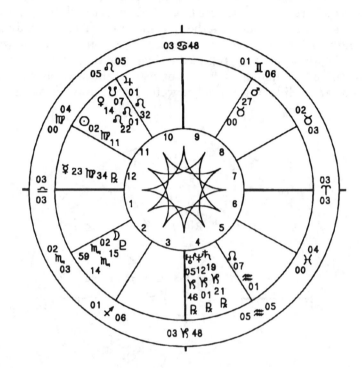

Example Chart #44:
25 Aug 1990 8:49 am PDT Coeur d'Alene, ID 47N41 116W46
"Is it safe to have sex with Leon?"

This is obviously an 8th house question, but the 7th (representing Leon) has to be taken into consideration as well. A lady who had met the gentleman of the question on a cruise had called from a port stop to ask this question. In these days with sexually transmitted diseases running rampant, it certainly is a valid query.

She is ruled by Venus at 14 Leo in the 11th; the ruler of the 8th is also Venus. Venus is not dignified, in detriment or fall, nor is it in a sign it rules. Its aspects are squares to Pluto and Mars and a quincunx to Saturn, none of them very reassuring for any kind of relationship, especially sexual. Since Mars at 27 Leo rules Leon (the 7th house) and Venus squares it, the answer is "no." The Moon at almost 3 Scorpio squares Venus and opposes Mars and will conjunct Pluto at 15 Scorpio. In this case Moon/Pluto is not a positive aspect, so the Moon's action confirms the "no" answer.

This is a case of the querent asking a question after the fact. When she called back for the answer, she was not happy with it as she had already entered into a sexual relationship with Leon. Every Horary astrologer will run into instances like this. You do the chart and give an answer to which the querent either pays no heed or has already acted upon and is asking you for reassurance. Often your judgment will be confirmed by later activity, but at the time, it is very frustrating. This case continued. Although, so far, it seems that the sex was safe, other 8th house areas did not work out so well. See the next question.

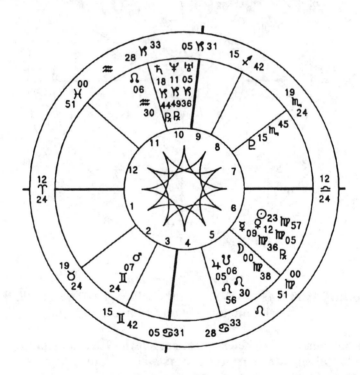

Example Chart #45:
16 Sep 1990 7:28 pm PDT Coeur d'Alene, ID 47N41 116W46
"Will Leon send me the money he owes me?
Will he come to see me? Will he contact me?"

This is a follow-up to the previous chart. When the querent got home, she expected to hear from Leon, to have him visit her and repay a loan she had advanced. More than two weeks had passed and she was becoming concerned.

Leon is signified by Venus at 12 Virgo, ruling the 7th and placed in the 6th (his 12th).

Both the querent (1st house) and the money he owes her (8th house) are ruled by Mars at 7 Gemini. Venus is past the square to Mars and

Mars quincunxes Pluto at 15 Scorpio, co-ruler of the 8th of money owed. It doesn't look like she will get the money back from him (square) nor that much will happen (quincunx). Jupiter at 5 Leo rules his house of communication and makes no aspect to Mars that rules her, so it is unlikely she will hear from him. The Moon which co-rules the question is at 0 Virgo, and will eventually conjunct Venus which rules him, thus it is doubtful he will come to visit her (the Moon rules her 4th). As previously stated the planets overrule the Moon. To date, he hasn't shown up nor has the money.

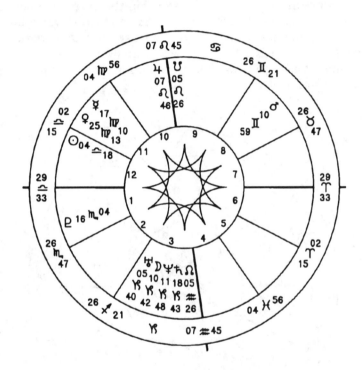

Example Chart #46:
27 Sep 1990 9:03 am PDT Coeur d'Alene, ID 47N41 116W46
"Is this a good time to transfer my funds to a Swiss bank?"

With 29 degrees Libra rising, it looks like the querent, despite asking the question, has already decided. Mars at 11 Gemini in the 8th and Pluto at 16 Scorpio rule his money (2nd house) and the 9th house, signifying distant Switzerland, is ruled by Mercury dignified at 17 Virgo. Venus at 25 Virgo rules him and Mercury is applying to a conjunction of Venus. The Moon at 10 Capricorn ruling the interception in the 9th house will trine both Mercury and Venus, and sextile Pluto. The answer is "yes."

11th And 12th House Questions

The 11th and 12th houses are rarely used as a focus for questions. People don't often ask if they will be committed to a mental institution, but if they do, you place the question in the 12th house. If you were asked, "When will I get out of the hospital?" you would consider the rulers of the 1st (the querent) and the 12th representing the hospital. Since the 12th is the house of large animals, answers to questions concerning horses or cows are found here. When using the derivative house system, the 12th represents the partner's 6th and thus comes into play when replying to questions about your spouse's health or work.

The 11th house is referred to when answering questions about friends, business income (as the 2nd from the 10th), groups or organizations and social events.

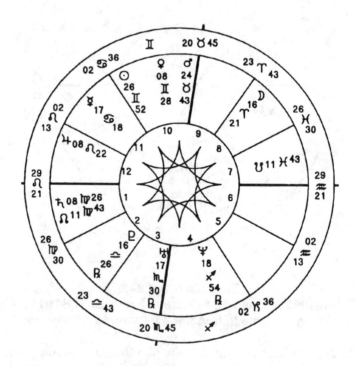

Example Chart #47:
Jun 18, 1979 10:15 am PDT Coeur d'Alene, ID 47N41 116W46
"Will my friend come to visit this summer?"

When we moved to Idaho in 1977, my daughter Bridget's girlfriend came with us to spend the summer. Two years later the girls were looking forward to spending the summer together again and my daughter asked this question.

Bridget's friend is depicted by the ruler of the 11th house which is the Moon at 16 Aries in the 8th house. The 4th house signifies our home, and is ruled by Mars at 24 Taurus in the 10th and Pluto at 16 Libra in the 2nd. The Moon applies to an exact opposition to Pluto which says "no." The Moon also squares Mercury at 17 Cancer in the 11th, another "no" answer. Though Bridget was disappointed that her friend would not come for the summer, she was able to make other plans on the strength of the Horary answer.

WHERE DID I PUT IT? IT CAN'T BE LOST!

Finding Lost Items

Horary Astrology can answer many different questions about many areas of life, but one of the easiest and most successful applications seems to be finding lost items. Everyone loses something now and then and this can be a very frustrating experience. Ancient astrological methods differ in the ways to locate lost belongings. Some say that all lost items come out of the 2nd house; others feel the 4th house is a better significator of possessions; some aver that whatever planet rules the item (Sun for gold, Moon for silver, Mars for metal, Mercury for books, etc.) is the way to go. Over the years, by trial and error I have determined the method that works for me. This streamlined technique speeds up the process and has served in locating myriad lost articles.

Rules For Finding Lost Items

1. All lost items are located from the sign on the cusp of the 2nd house, its ruler and any planets in this house. (Dispositors may be used.) The 2nd house reflects your belongings.

If the questioner has lost the item, go directly to the 2nd house and judge the answer from that perspective. If however, the querent asks, "Where did my son leave his wallet?" you would look to the 6th house, which is the 2nd from the 5th representing the son. If the question refers to the husband's wallet, the 2nd from the 7th (husband) is the 8th (his wallet). In interpreting the chart for the lost item, it is necessary to know what is lost and **WHO** lost it. This is an application of the derivative house system. When you do Horary Astrology, you learn a great deal about houses in the chart.

If the person who asks the question refers to someone else by NAME, use the 7th house to identify the person and the 8th to define her/his lost item.

2. Where you find the ruler of the 2nd house is the first place to look for the lost object. The **sign and house** of that planet will provide clues.

Clues may relate to areas inside a house or outdoors. They may suggest colors or directions. You must consider all the clues and use common sense and logic regarding which ones you pass on to a client.

For the first question, "Where is my wallet?" locate the ruler of the 2nd house. If the ruler is in the 3rd house of the chart, look in the car or garage, ask your sister or brother, or look in the den or library (any place where there are books or papers). [See **Houses** list which follows.]

If the ruler is in the 8th house, look in the bathroom, kitchen or laundry room (any place where there are pipes or plumbing).

3. The signs also describe possible places where lost items may be located. (See Lost Item Reference Table which follows.) Besides reading the sign of the ruler of the 2nd house, you can consider the location of the dispositor of that sign for added information.

For the "Where is my wallet?" question, if the ruler of the 2nd house is in Aries, the wallet might be near heat, such as a stove, fireplace, furnace, or chimney. It may be near the ceiling or upper part of a room.

Obviously, it is imperative that the astrologer has a solid understanding of the meanings of signs and houses.

4. Directions are judged from the actual directions in the chart. Planets on the Ascendant are east; on the Descendant side, west; near the Midheaven, south; near the 4th house cusp, north. (Refer to Table of Directions in Lesson III on page 13 or the **Houses** table which follows.)

If the 2nd house ruler is in the 3rd house, the wallet may be in a northeast section of the house. If the ruler of the 2nd is in the 8th house, the wallet could be in the southwestern area of the house.

5. Colors can sometimes be significant in locating lost articles. They relate to both planets and signs in horary astrology.

If the 2nd house ruler is the Moon in Aries, the lost wallet might be near something white, cream, or silver (the Moon) or white and red (Aries). [See the table relating colors to signs and planets which follows.]

6. The Part of Fortune. I'm a nuts-and-bolts astrologer who sticks mainly to the planets, signs and houses in natal astrology. But in lost item Horary, I find the Part of Fortune to be very helpful. It is often a secondary indicator of where to look. I always figure the Part of Fortune from the original chart. Even if you turn the chart, or renumber the houses to read it, I find it more accurate to calculate *Pars Fortuna* from the original Ascendant. There is disagreement about this among astrologers so try it for yourself but this works best for me.

Lost item charts are the only place where I use the Part of Fortune and it is invariably a clue. Consider its sign and house position and also the planet that disposits it in looking for direction, color and distance.

Though I renumber or turn the chart to interpret, "Where did my son leave his wallet?" and use the 5th house (son) as the Ascendant, I still figure the Part of Fortune from the original Ascendant, not the 5th house cusp.

7. Retrograde planets are more meaningful in Lost Item Horary than any other astrological charts that I work with.

It is rare that an astrological aphorism **always** works, but one that rarely misses is that if the lost item is signified by a retrograde planet, it will be returned or found.

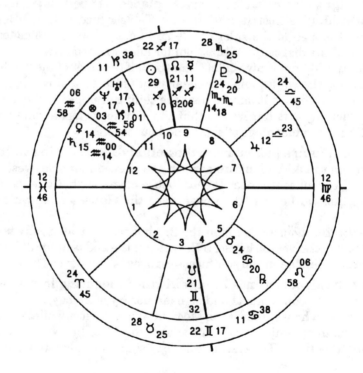

Example Chart #48:
20 Dec 1992 11:15 am PST Coeur d'Alene, ID 47N41 116W46
"Where is my sweater?"

A client went to the closet to get her favorite sweater and it was no-where to be found, so I was the recipient of a frantic phone call. Mars rules her 2nd house, the sweater, and it is retrograde, which seems to promise she will find it. Its 5th house placement suggests that since she doesn't have children (a typical 5th house location... child's room) that she may have left it someplace where she was having fun... a party, at her boyfriend's house, at a restaurant or a theater. The Part of Fortune as well as its dispositor, Uranus, is in the 11th, confirming that she may have been out with friends or left it at a club, or group meeting, even at someone's house.

As soon as I said this, she remembered that it was in the bedroom closet at a friend's home. She had removed it because she was warm, and being careful with her clothes she had put it in a safe place.

8. **Dispositors are very significant when searching for a mis-placed article.** Not only will the 2nd house ruler and the Part of Fortune provide clues, so will their dispositors, especially as to color and direction.

9. **If the planet ruling the lost item is in Virgo, Pisces, the 6th or 12th house, it is usually not visible and may be found in a draw-er, cupboard, pocket or some other enclosed place.**

LOST ITEM REFERENCE TABLE

Following is a list of places where lost items may be found, using the signs and houses for location. If the ruler of the lost item is going out of one sign into the next, chances are the missing article is behind something.

SIGNS

If the significator of the lost item is in:

FIRE: Near heat such as a stove, furnace, fireplace or chimney. In the upper part of the room.

ARIES: Near sandy or hilly ground, unfrequented places. In houses, near the ceiling. Outside, near or in stables, plowed land.

LEO: Woods, forests, deserts, rocky places, parks, ovens.

SAGITTARIUS: Stables, barns, hills and high lands. Libraries, upper floors of a house.

EARTH: Near floor or pavement, in cellar or basement, or underground.

TAURUS: Barns, warehouses, bushes, basements, or first floor of a house. Banks or where money is kept.

VIRGO: Studies, libraries, bookcases, closets, gardens, pantries, offices. Often not visible, in a pocket, drawer or cupboard.

CAPRICORN: At work, parent's home, bushy, barren or thorny places. In dark corners near the ground, farming areas or mines.

AIR: Up high, possibly outside hanging on a line or in a tree.

GEMINI: Near a wall, wainscoting, in a chest or trunk. Dining room, schoolroom or other place of learning. In the car, garage or nursery.

LIBRA: Attics, bedrooms, mountain tops, hills, outside in the clear, sharp air.

AQUARIUS: Hilly, uneven ground. Vineyards, roofs, windows. Lecture halls, airplanes.

WATER: Near plumbing, dairies, kitchens, lakes, rivers, ponds, fountains, near water of any kind.

CANCER: Brooks, springs, sinks, kitchens, wells, sea shores, restaurants, cooking areas. The back yard.

SCORPIO: Dirty places, drains, swamps, trash bins, marshes, orchards.

PISCES: Springs, rivers or ponds with fish. Old houses, cisterns, wells, places of seclusion or hidden.

HOUSES

If the significator of the lost item is in the:

1ST HOUSE: It is usually where the person who owns it put it and unless the ruler of the house is seriously afflicted (squares and oppositions), the item will be retrieved or returned. This house represents the place where the querent spends the most time, also the entry hall, front porch, front door and windows of a house.

DIRECTION: East

2ND HOUSE: Where money or precious things are kept; in a bank or vault or safety deposit box. The bedroom, boudoir, furnishings, flower garden, shrubbery.

DIRECTION: North by East

3RD HOUSE: In the car or garage. A sibling may have it or know where it is. In a desk or where letters or books are kept. At a store or market. The TV or media room, study, desk, hallway, and stairway. Busses, taxis. Homes of siblings or neighbors. Schools.

DIRECTION: Northeast.

4TH HOUSE: At home, in the kitchen or pantry. In a safe, secure place. In the garden or yard. At a parent's home. Basement, dining room, sinks, water pipes. Any place food is stored. Restaurants. The beach.

DIRECTION: North

5TH HOUSE: A child may have put it somewhere or know where it is. In a child's room, bar, theater, the ball park, playground, den, game room, any place of pleasure or enjoyment. The racetrack, casino, stock market. The heating system, fireplace or hearth in the home.

DIRECTION: North by West

6TH HOUSE: At work or someone at work may have it or have seen it or put it someplace. A pet may have dragged it away. In a box, pocket, drawer or cabinet. Where you keep clothes, or in the linen closet. Often out of sight. Grocery stores, restaurants, zoos. Doctors', lawyers' or agents' offices. The sewing room or studio in the home.

DIRECTION: Northwest

7TH HOUSE: Partner may have seen it or put it somewhere. Bedroom, living room, formal dining room, patio or porch. Usually in plain sight. The partner's room, office or place of business.

DIRECTION: West

8TH HOUSE: Totally out of sight, often unrecoverable. Check any place where there is plumbing; bathroom, kitchen, basement. Cemeteries, insurance companies, laboratories.

DIRECTION: South by West

9TH HOUSE: At school, on an airplane or long trip. Usually indicates item is far away. Church, library. Attic, high shelves, stables, college, and university.

DIRECTION: Southwest

10TH HOUSE: Hall, study, dining room, public building, department store, or place of business; a parent or boss may know where it is. The house foundation, floors, roof, joists, walls, structure in general.

DIRECTION: South

11TH HOUSE: A meeting place, lodge or clubhouse. A friend may have seen it or put it someplace. Any work area in the home.

DIRECTION: South by East

12TH HOUSE: Whatever the lost item is, it is out of sight, thoroughly hidden and often undetectable. It could be in the doctor's office, the hospital or infirmary.

DIRECTION: Southeast.

Sometimes certain areas or items are represented by more than one house, *e.g.*, bedrooms are found in both the 2nd and the 5th houses.

COLORS RELATING TO SIGNS AND PLANETS

SIGNS		PLANETS	
Aries	- White w/red	Moon	- White/cream/silver
Taurus	- White w/lemon	Mercury	- Light blue/dove
Gemini	- White w/orange	Venus	- White/purple
Cancer	- Green/russet	Sun	- Yellow/purple/gold
Leo	- Red or green	Mars	- Fiery red
Virgo	- Black speckled	Jupiter	- Red mixed w/green
Libra	- Pastel colors	Ash	
Scorpio	- Brown	Saturn	- Black/green
Sagittarius	- Yellow/green	Uranus	- Plaids/checks/mingled
Capricorn	- Black/dark brown	Neptune	- Turquoise/sea colors
Aquarius	- Sky blue	Pluto	- Dark hues generally
Pisces	- Turquoise		

COMPOUND COLORS

☽/☿	- Buff or fawn	☿/♀	- Purple or light mix
☽/♀	- Light blue/bluish white	☿/☉	- Light gray
☽/☉	- Light yellow or green	☿/♂	- Red or brick color
☽/♂	- Light glistening red	☿/♃	- Spotted green
☽/♃	- Bright green	☿/♄	- Dark blue-gray
☽/♄	- Russet or gray	☿/♅	- Light blue plaids
☽/♅	- Fine checked plaid	☿/♆	- Grayed blue or denim
☽/♆	- Aqua	☿/♇	- Grayed deep tones
☽/♇	- Brown		(Mauve/taupe)

♀/☉	- Olive	☉/♂	- Coral
♀/♂	- Light red or pink	☉/♃	- Deep, shiny red
♀/♃	- Lavender/heliotrope	☉/♄	- Blackish orange/bronze
♀/♄	- Light blue gray	☉/♅	- Green & purple plaids
♀/♅	- Blue & white plaid	☉/♆	- Green/blue mixtures
♀/♆	- Purple & blue print	☉/♇	- Deep purple
♀/♇	- Soft, dark colors		

♂/♃	- Tan/brown mixture	♃/♄	- Dark green with black & brown
♂/♄	- Dark red/brown	♃/♅	- Green & red plaids
♂/♅	- Red plaids	♃/♆	- Grayed turquoise/green
♂/♆	- Deep purple mixture	♃/♇	- Dark ash tones
♂/♇	- Blood red		

		♅/♆	- Turquoise & dark blue plaids
♄/♅	- Green plaid	♅/♇	- Dark brown & black plaids
♄/♆	- Murky green/blue		
♄/♇	- Black mixtures	♆/♇	- Burgundy

Charts To Learn From

The following examples of lost article situations were solved by the foregoing rules.

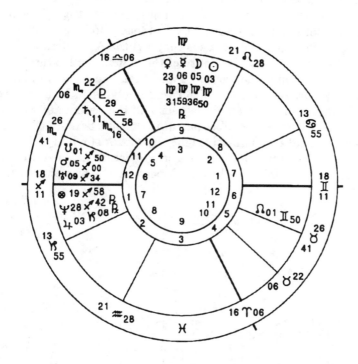

Example Chart #49:
26 Aug 1984 3:25 pm PDT Coeur d'Alene, ID 47N41 116W46
"Where is Jim's billfold?"

A client called and asked this question about her son's wallet. She called him specifically by name, which according to my rules indicates the 7th house as the owner of the lost article. If she had said "Where is my son's billfold?" I would have used the 5th house for her son and the 6th as representative of his wallet, but since she referred to him by name, he became a 7th house person. See Rule 1 on pages 78-79. There is a great deal of disagreement about this by Horary astrologers. Some feel that if you know the relationship, you should immediately use the corresponding house. I have found that the 7th house designation works best if the person is called by name. If the questioner refers to the individual as "my cousin," "my son," "my mother," etc., I use the corresponding house that describes the relationship. My technique works well for me, but you should try both systems and decide which works best for you.

Remember, once you decide, be consistent. **Consistency breeds accuracy.**

In this chart Mercury at 7 Virgo rules the 7th house; the Moon at 5 Virgo rules his 2nd house (8th of the chart). Mercury is in his 3rd and this placement of the lost wallet ruler suggests that it is in a car, garage, near books or papers, but since the Moon is in Virgo, it is probably out of sight. The Part of Fortune is conjunct the Ascendant and its dispositor, Jupiter is in the 1st house of the chart. I called her back and told her where the wallet could be and that I thought he must have found it by now because the Moon was applying to a conjunction of Mercury within one and a half degrees and the Ascendant was within less than a degree of *Pars Fortuna* which meant hours, not days. She laughed and said I was exactly right. Just after she had called me, he found the billfold underneath a book on cars which he had been reading in the den. She hadn't called me back because she was embarrassed.

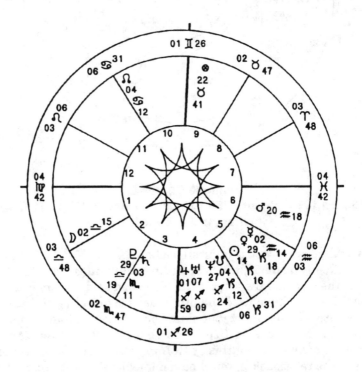

Example Chart #50:
4 Jan 1983 8:41 pm PST Las Vegas, NV 36N10 115W09
"Where is my cat?"

An astrologer I didn't know called and asked this question about a very dear pet. She had set up the chart when she asked the question where she lived at her local time. Ordinarily, I set up the chart when and where I hear and understand the question, but in this case, because she felt better about using her chart, I used her time and coordinates.

The 6th house represents pets and the ruler here is Uranus at 7 Sagittarius in the 4th house. This indicates that the cat is far away (Sagittarius), north of where the woman is (4th house), near a stable in hilly or high land. The Part of Fortune is in the 9th house confirming the faraway location. Since Mercury, ruler of the 1st house at 2 Aquarius representing the astrologer, sextiles Uranus (ruler of her pet) in five degrees, it seemed likely she would get the cat back in five days or five weeks. The Moon, co-ruler of the question, is at 2 Libra and also sextiles Uranus in five degrees and trines Mercury, confirming that she will get the cat back and verifying the timing.

When looking for timing try to find as many aspects as possible to confirm. Jupiter at 2 Sagittarius rules the 4th house and conjuncts Uranus (cat) in five degrees. The cat was found almost five weeks later in a stable on a ranch about 12 to 15 miles north of where the woman lived.

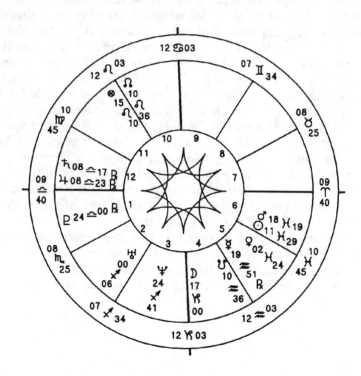

Example Chart #51:
1 March 1981 8:00 pm PST Coeur d'Alene, ID 47N41 116W46
"Where are my airline tickets?"

A friend had put her tickets away for safekeeping and the evening before her flight was leaving, she couldn't find them. Needless to say, I
was the recipient of a frantic phone call. Mars and Pluto both represent
the tickets (co-rulers of the 2nd house). Mars is at 18 Pisces in the 6th
house indicating that they are out of sight (Pisces) in a cupboard or
drawer (6th house). Pluto is retrograde in the 1st house at 24 Libra; she
will get them back (Pluto retrograde) and they are close by (1st house)
and where she put them. Neptune, the dispositor of Mars, is in the 3rd
house at 24 Sagittarius suggesting they are around papers or books.
The Moon, co-ruler of the question, is in the 4th house at 17 Capricorn
indicating that the kitchen is a possible place to look. The Part of Fortune is in the 11th in Leo disposited by the Sun in Pisces in the 6th,
reaffirming the original assumption that they were in a drawer or cabinet. She called back shortly after receiving this information and said
that her child (*Pars Fortuna* in Leo of children) had found the tickets in
a drawer of the kitchen desk beneath the phone (3rd house).

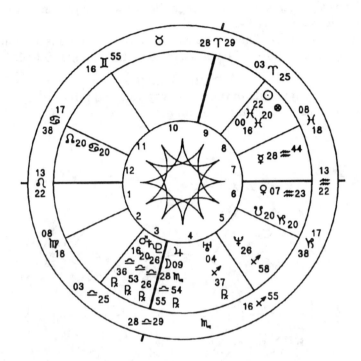

Example Chart #52:
12 Mar 1982 2:12 pm PST Coeur d'Alene, ID 47N41 116W46
"Where is my coat?"

A friend (same one) called and said the last time she had seen her suede coat, she had tossed it in the back seat of the car. A couple of days later she needed it, but it wasn't there. Her coat is ruled by Mercury (Virgo on the 2nd) at 28 Aquarius in the 7th house. The dispositor is Uranus retrograde at 4 Sagittarius in the 4th. *Pars Fortuna* is in the 8th at 20 Pisces and the dispositor is in the 5th. These clues suggest that her husband (7th) may have put the coat someplace and perhaps a child (dispositor of the Part of Fortune in the 5th) would know where it was. She called her husband at work; he was at lunch and her daughter was in school and couldn't be contacted. When her husband came home that night he knew exactly where he put the coat. It was in the closet in her daughter's bedroom, because he thought it was their daughter's coat.

To find lost items, animals or even people using Horary charts, just follow the rules and proceed logically. Encourage people to ask the question when they FIRST think of it. Sometimes a chart is difficult to read because the question isn't timed correctly (asked too soon or too late).

This is a great way to become involved with Horary Astrology because it is relatively simple and you will get better with experience. Remember, practice makes perfect.

A reference table for lost items including signs, houses, colors as well as rooms and parts of houses can be found on pages 82-84.

Missing People

You find missing people in the same way you find missing objects, but you use the 7th rather than the 2nd house.

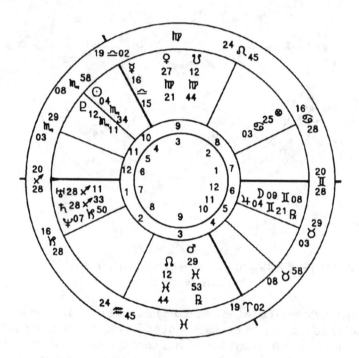

Example Chart #53:
27 Oct 1988 11:32 am PDT Coeur d'Alene, ID 47N41 116W46
"Where is Karen?"

A client in Los Angeles called and asked where this mentally disturbed young woman was. She had been staying with an aunt and had said she was going back home. When she didn't arrive, her parents were very upset, but because she was of age and hadn't been gone over 24 hours, the police couldn't do anything.

Karen is Mercury, ruler of the 7th house (renumber), in her 3rd house (9th of the chart) at 16 Libra. The Moon, co-ruler of the question, as well as dispositor of *Pars Fortuna* (25 Cancer), is in her 12th at 9

Gemini, trine Mercury suggesting that she is alive and okay...but where? The 3rd house indicates local area, Libra is hills or high country. Mercury sextiles Uranus and Saturn at 28 Sagittarius, verifying that she was safe. With the Moon in her 12th, she was hiding and didn't want to be found. There is no aspect between Mercury which rules her and Venus, ruler of her home, so I doubted she would return of her own volition. The direction indicated is North and East, her significator, Mercury in her 3rd.

She was staying with friends in Lancaster in the high desert of California which is northeast of her home in Santa Monica. My client, who was a friend of the parents, went there and brought her home.

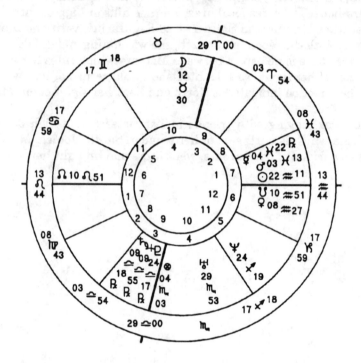

Example Chart #54:
10 Feb 1981 4:11 pm PST Coeur d'Alene, ID 47N41 116W46
"Where is Millicent? If she's dead, where is her body?"

The sheriff from a neighboring county called me and asked this question. He didn't want anyone to know that he "believed" in astrology, so he swore me to secrecy. The woman had last been seen in a popular bar in the small town where she lived, but hadn't returned home and some friends were worried about her.

She is represented by Uranus, ruler of the 7th house. It is in her 10th house in the 29th degree of Scorpio, suggesting that she was, at the very least, at the end of her rope. The Sun at 22 Aquarius in her 1st house squares Uranus, not very reassuring. Her 8th and 4th houses are ruled by Mercury at 4 Pisces and Mars at 3 Pisces which both trine Uranus, giving a "yes" answer to the 2nd question. With these significators all in water signs, it would seem she had drowned or would be found in a watery place. With intercepted Venus, co-ruler of the 4th (her 10th) in her 12th at 8 Aquarius square Uranus, it seemed her body would be found in a southerly direction (Uranus and the Part of Fortune in her 10th), but the Moon in her 4th gives the opposite direction.

When I gave the sheriff the description of Scorpio places (marshy, where there were trash bins or dumps) and Taurus places (barns, warehouses, underground), he thought he might know where she was. He then asked, after the fact, whether there had been foul play. I explained to him that it was almost impossible to judge that after the question had been asked.

Her body was found in a shallow river north and east of her home many months later. Her car was never found, but to this day no one has been arrested in connection with her death. If you use the directions calculated from the turned chart, you would expect to have found her south (Uranus, her significator, in 10th house of the turned chart). Instead, by using the chart as calculated as I advocate in Rule 4 for finding lost items on page 79, the Part of Fortune and Uranus, both in the 4th, point in a northerly direction.

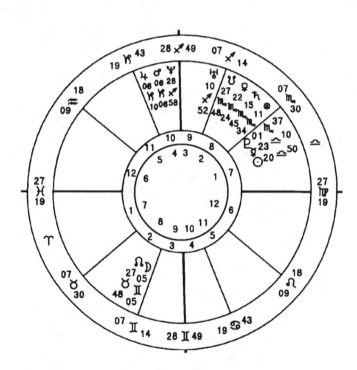

Example Chart #55:
13 Oct 1984 5:11 pm PDT Coeur d'Alene, ID 47N41 116W46
"When will Ginny be found or return?"

A student's seventeen-year-old daughter had run away from home and her mother was extremely concerned about her.

Ginny is represented by Mercury, ruler of the 7th (her 1st, because we have renumbered the houses) at 23 Libra in her 1st house. Her home is ruled by Jupiter at 6 Capricorn and there is no aspect between those two planets. However, co-ruler Moon at 5 Gemini will quincunx Jupiter in the 4th and trine Mercury so she will definitely return home. This is an example of the translation and collection of light. (See Rule 6 on page 6.) But her mother had asked when, not if, she would come back. Mercury sextiles Neptune in her 4th house in approximately six degrees and the Moon trines Mercury in 18 degrees. The Moon is Mutable/Succedent, Mercury is Cardinal/Angular and Neptune is Mutable/Angular so it looks as though the timing would be relatively fast. I told the mother she would return in six to 18 days. She came home 12 days later.

COMPOUND AND MULTIPLE QUESTIONS

WHO, WHERE, WHAT, WHEN, WHY & HOW?

As mentioned earlier you can answer several questions with one chart, as long as they are all asked at the same time. They may all refer to the same subject or involve different topics. I refer to these as compound or multiple questions.

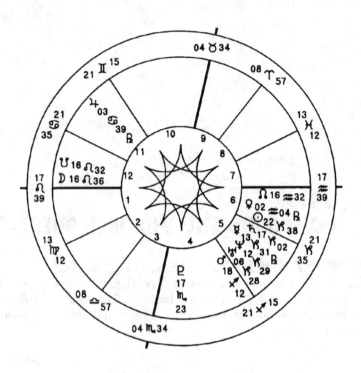

Example Chart #56:
12 Jan 1990 6:27 pm PST Coeur d'Alene, ID 47N41 116W46
"Should Pam and I become business partners? Should my
husband and I move to California? Is it financially feasible?"

A client who lived on the East coast called with this compound question. It was a difficult question to answer, because Pam and the client's
husband both show up in the 7th house.

The querent is the Sun at 22 Capricorn (business) in the 6th house
(work)... a valid chart. She wanted to know if she should go into business with a partner. Uranus at 6 Capricorn rules her 7th and Venus at
2 Aquarius is the ruler of the business 10th. There is no aspect between
the Sun and Uranus or Venus, so the business idea seems unlikely to
work out. Both the Sun and Uranus apply to the second question as
well, since Uranus (ruler of the 7th) also represents her husband. The
ruler of the 9th (long distance move) is Mars at 18 Sagittarius which is
in the 4th house (their current home), making no aspect to Pluto which
is also there. It looks highly unlikely that they will be making a long
distance home change very soon. So the financial part of the question

becomes unnecessary to answer. The business opportunity fell through and the couple decided to stay where they were.

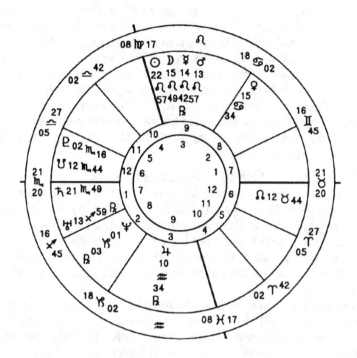

Example Chart #57:
15 Aug 1985 1:50 pm PDT Coeur d'Alene, ID 47N41 116W46
"Should Ben go into the service? Should we buy Nikki (horse)?
Should we move to Boise?"

The daughter of a friend called with this multiple question. As always, it is important to decide how you will approach the chart, before you start to answer the question. Ben will be represented by the 7th house. The service is both 6th and 7th. The horse is found in the 12th of large animals. For the move we must consider both 4th and 9th.

To answer the question about Ben, it is necessary to renumber the houses, so we'll answer that one last. Before turning the chart, we must answer the other questions. "Should we buy Nikki?" Mars at 14 Leo and Pluto at 2 Scorpio rule the 1st house and Venus at 15 Cancer rules the 12th (the horse). There is no aspect between Mars or Pluto and Venus. Saturn is rising suggesting a "no" answer. About the long distance move, Neptune at 1 Capricorn rules their current home (4th) and the Moon at 15 Leo rules the 9th. There is no aspect from the Moon to Neptune, indicating that this is probably not a good time for a move.

When we renumber the chart, Ben (indicated by the 7th) is ruled by Venus and his 6th house (12th of the chart) is also ruled by Venus in the 8th house (his 2nd). His 7th house is ruled by Mars and Pluto, the same planets involved in the question about the horse. Again we have no connection, so most likely the action will not be taken. When she called for the answer, she admitted that all of it was a kind of pipe dream. They were both unhappy with their jobs and were looking for changes. She agreed that buying a horse when money was tight would be foolish. Neptune in the 2nd doesn't always view money sensibly. About three months later he got a very good job, she got pregnant and their lives took an upward turn.

Other Considerations

In many cases, two planets in Mutual Reception work toward a yes answer (see Rule 12 on page 8), but I do not base my answer solely on this. Any planet that is dignified or exalted carries extra weight, while one in detriment or fall can often have a negative effect on the answer. Be sure to consider signs that are intercepted in the house and look to their rulers for more information in connection with the question and answer.

In some cases when there is no aspect between the ruler of the querent and the house of the question, the Moon may be aspecting first one of the planets and then the other. This is called **translation and collection of light**. (See Rule 6 on page 6.) This is how it works: the question is, "Will Tom propose to me?" Assume the ruler of the Ascendant (the questioner) is Mars at 16 degrees of Aquarius; the ruler of the 7th house (Tom) is Venus at 24 degrees Aries; there is no aspect (no action). But the Moon at 12 Gemini will trine Mars and then sextile Venus, certainly indicating the potential of a yes answer. In this case, the Moon aspects first Mars, then Venus, translating and collecting the light — thus connecting the two planets.

All aspects must be applying to have an effect on the answer. However, if the aspect is less than one degree past, I have learned that you can use it. For example, if Mercury rules the querent and Jupiter rules the question and Mercury is at 26 Virgo 49 minutes and Jupiter is at 25 Virgo 50 minutes, you can still count it as a conjunction.

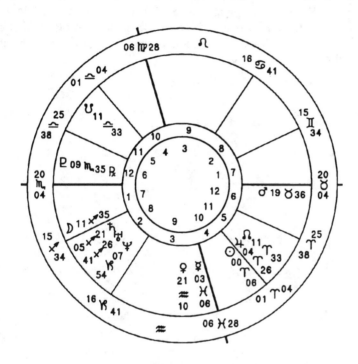

Example Chart #58:
20 March 1987 10:27 pm PST Coeur d'Alene, ID 47N41 116W46
"If Chris goes to trial, will he win?"

Chris was involved in an accident claim and was being sued. His girlfriend asked the question.

Either renumber the houses or turn the chart. Chris is ruled by Venus, ruler of the 7th at 21 Aquarius. Saturn at 21 Sagittarius and Uranus at 26 Sagittarius rule his 9th (3rd of the chart). Venus is just past (five minutes) a sextile to Saturn and it will also sextile Uranus. The Moon at 11 Sagittarius conjuncts Saturn and then sextiles Venus (translation and collection of light). Yes, he will go to trial. In judging whether he will win, you have to take into consideration his opponent who is represented by the 1st house of the chart (which is Chris' 7th house of open enemies). The 1st house has Scorpio on the cusp, ruled by Mars at 19 Taurus and Pluto at 9 Scorpio. Venus, representing Chris, has better aspects to Saturn, ruler of Chris' 9th house, than Mars has to his opponent's 9th house, which is ruled by the Moon at 11 Virgo and the Sun (Leo is intercepted in the 9th) at 0 Aries. The Moon quincunxes

Mars and makes no aspect to Pluto; the Sun quincunxes Pluto and makes no aspect to Mars... not very favorable for his opponent. The Moon will conjunct Saturn and Uranus, rulers of Chris' 9th house, and the Sun trines both planets. The outcome looked favorable for Chris — he should win. He did.

AND THE WINNER IS...

CONTEST CHARTS

My first experience with judging contests with Horary Astrology happened when my eight-year-old son asked an astrologer friend if UCLA would win a crucial basketball game. She set up a chart for the moment he asked and said they would... and they did. Naturally, all the sports fans in the neighborhood immediately became entranced with this "voodoo" we did at the kitchen table. We spent many hours casting charts for the onset of basketball, football and baseball games, but it profited us little. It seems there must be an urgent need to know or a personal involvement before this type of question can be answered successfully. Chart #34 (page 62) is a good example. The coach was very much involved with the outcome of the game, so the question was important to her and therefore a viable one.

Every Horary Astrologer will eventually be confronted with this type of question and the following rules apply.

1. **Make sure this is not an idle question** but one which has meaning to the querent.

2. **If the question is "Will the (name of team) win tonight?"** use **the 7th house to represent the team** and the 1st house to designate their opponents.

3. **Determine the outcome by comparing the aspects between each team's 5th house** (how they play the game) **and their 10th house**, indicating their honor and ability to win.

This takes careful consideration and the astrologer must set up a kind of score sheet to keep track of which team has the edge. If the results are very close, it could be a very close score and the winner may be hard to determine. If one team clearly outclasses the other (astrologically), that team will usually be the winner. This is not as easy as it sounds. I have had some resounding victories but also some duds.

I have not been successful when I set up a chart for the beginning of a game and try to judge which team will win. Other astrologers have good results, but they differ on which house represents the home team and which one is the visitor. I get the best results when asking about a specific competitor and whether s/he or they will win. This is another area of Horary Astrology where the Part of Fortune seems to be relevant, but only as a confirmation.

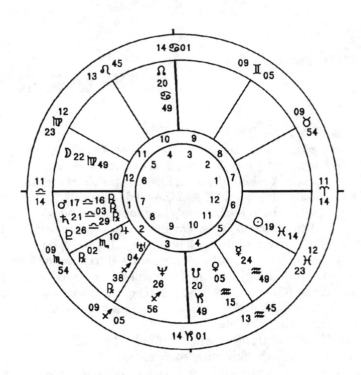

Example Chart #59:
9 Mar 1982 7:38 pm PST Coeur d'Alene, ID 47N41 116W46
"Will the Vandals win the playoff game?"

My husband and son are avid sports fans, so I get many of these questions from them. Our home team had a pretty good chance to win the whole tournament, hence this question.

The Vandals are represented by the 7th house, so it is necessary to renumber or turn the chart. Their honor is their 10th (4th of the chart); their 5th is the way they will play the game. Mars at 17 Libra rules them and is in their 7th (the opponent's 1st) and conjuncts Saturn the ruler of their 10th. Venus at 5 Aquarius, ruler of the opponents, is in their 10th house and trines Mars and Saturn. The Part of Fortune at 14 Aries is in their 1st house, a promising position. When I looked at the chart, I had a difficult time deciding if the two malefics representing the Vandals boded ill for them. I concluded that since both Mars and Saturn were in the 1st house of the opponents, they would not win, therefore the Vandals would. They did... in overtime, 69 to 67.

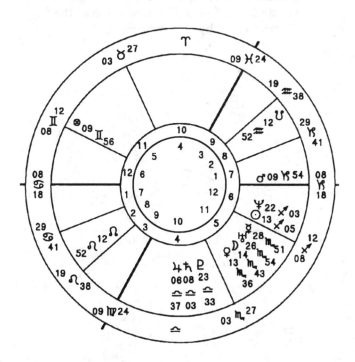

Example Chart #60:
4 Dec 1980 5:35 pm Coeur d'Alene, ID 47N41 116W46
"Is Houston going to win tonight?"

This is another of those "urgent, need to know" sport charts. Houston is depicted by the 7th house. Remember the person or team asked about is always placed in the 7th and you must turn or renumber the houses. In this case Saturn at 8 Libra rules Houston and is in their house of honor, the 10th (4th of the chart). Jupiter at 6 Libra will conjunct it, a positive aspect. Saturn is exalted in Libra, another plus. Venus rules their 5th house (11th of the chart) and doesn't offer much help, since it is in detriment in Scorpio and in the opponents 5th.

You must always look at the prospects of the opposing team to see who will receive the most honor (10th) and who will play the best game (5th). In this instance, the opposition team is ruled by the Moon which is in its fall at 14 Scorpio in that team's 5th house. The Moon is past the trine to their Midheaven and the Ascendant. Pluto at 23 Libra and Mars at almost 10 Capricorn rule their 5th. Pluto is not involved in any great aspects, but Mars very widely sextiles Uranus in their 5th so the competition could be close. With Jupiter in Houston's 10th and *Pars Fortuna* just barely in their 5th, it looked like Houston had the edge. It was a close game, but Houston won by a narrow margin.

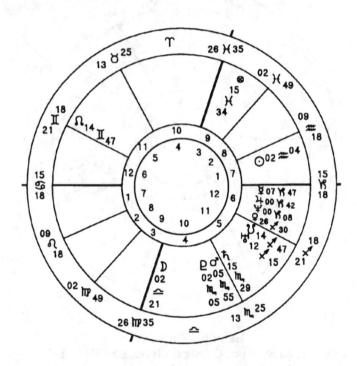

Example Chart #61:
22 Jan 1984 4:00 pm Kansas City, MO 39N06 94W35
"Will the Redskins win the Superbowl?"

I had lectured on Horary Astrology in Kansas City this afternoon and during the break we were discussing contest charts. I asked the question because I knew my family would be interested and I would be talking to my husband that evening. One of the attendees ran the chart for me.

The Redskins are described by the 7th house, which is ruled by Saturn in the opponent's 5th at 15 Scorpio (not good). Their 5th house is ruled by Venus at 26 Sagittarius in their 12th (not good); their 10th is ruled by Mercury at 7 Capricorn, also in their 12th (again not good). Mercury sextiles Saturn (good). The Raiders, their opponents, are represented by the Moon at 2 Libra; their 10th is ruled by Neptune at 0 Capricorn, their 5th by Mars and Pluto in 5 and 2 Scorpio respectively. Though slightly past (17 minutes), the Moon (the Raiders' ruler) trines the Sun, and as previously stated, we will count it, ruler of their 2nd house in the Redskins' 1st, a definite edge for the Raiders. Neptune is still conjunct Jupiter (past by 34 minutes) in their 6th (good). The Part of Fortune on the home team (Redskins) side of the chart was not enough for them to win.

Although I hoped the Redskins would pull out a victory, it looked to me like the Raiders had the winning team. This was a difficult chart to be objective about. The Raiders won 38-9.

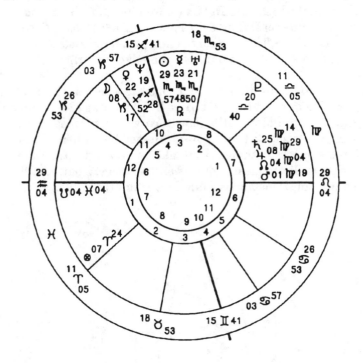

Example Chart #62:
22 Nov 1979 12:40 pm PST Coeur d'Alene, ID 47N41 116W46
"Will Dallas beat Houston?" "Will it snow tonight?"

A family group was watching football together on a chilly Sunday afternoon when one of the men asked the first question. One of the women asked if it would snow that evening. Though a compound question chart, it is included in this section since we are concerned here with contest charts.

Dallas, the first team named, is the 7th house ruled by the Sun at 29 Scorpio and Mercury at 23 Scorpio. Mercury (Virgo intercepted) also rules their 10th (the 4th of the chart) and Saturn at 25 Virgo rules their 5th. The Sun is in the last degree of Scorpio in their 4th house. The 29th degree of any sign, when it represents a person or group of people, often suggests being at the end of their rope. (This is a minus.) Mercury sextiles Saturn in their 1st which rules their 5th. This looks pretty good.

Let's look at Houston. It is represented by Uranus at almost 22 Scorpio in their 9th and Neptune at 19 Sagittarius in their 10th. Their 10th house is ruled by Jupiter at 8 Virgo in the 7th (the 1st house of Dallas), a plus for Houston. Their 5th is ruled by the Moon at 8 Capricorn, which trines Jupiter and sextiles Uranus before it sextiles Mercury and the Sun, which rule Dallas (more plusses for Houston). It also trines Saturn, ruler of Dallas' 5th (a plus for Dallas). *Pars Fortuna* is in Houston's 1st house. This is a confirming plus for Houston. It looks like a close game but that Houston has the edge, and that is the way it turned out.

As to the other question, when it comes to weather, the 6th house is the target. The querent is represented by Uranus at 22 Scorpio and the 6th is ruled by the Moon at 8 Capricorn which sextiles Uranus. The answer is yes. It snowed really hard. Remember, when Uranus is involved in the question, things often take an unusual turn. The weather bureau had predicted clearing skies and no snow. I batted a thousand on these two questions and my family was impressed, for a day or two.

UNIVERSAL QUESTIONS

STORMS, EARTHQUAKES AND WARS

When I first started studying Horary Astrology I read and was told by Horary astrologers that you could not answer what I refer to as "universal" questions. These are questions like "When will the war in Vietnam end?" "Will William Clinton win the election?" The reason given was that the questioner had no vested interest in the outcome of the question. I accepted this line of reasoning and for years eschewed this type of question.

However, a couple of occasions arose when someone insisted on an answer and I was surprised to discover that "universal" questions can indeed be answered. Of course, as with any Horary question, it needs to at least in some way be meaningful to the questioner.

In 1984 my husband, the sports nut, was disturbed that Russia might not participate in the Olympics and he asked the following question.

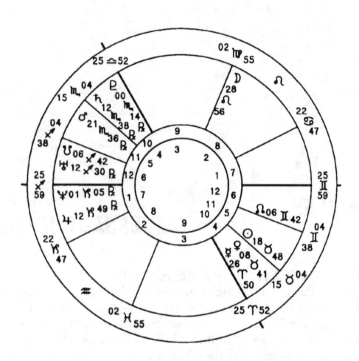

Example Chart #63:
8 May 1984 11:14 pm PDT Coeur d'Alene, ID 47N41 116W46
"Will the Russians come to the Olympics?"

The Russians are represented by the 7th house which is ruled by Mercury at 26 Aries in the 4th. I felt the Olympics were depicted by both the 10th (honor and prestige) and the 5th of games. They are both Venus-ruled and Mercury makes no aspect to Venus at 8 Taurus, suggesting not much action.

A student looking at the chart felt the question should be placed in the 4th house, as representative of the Olympic games being staged in this country. If we look at it that way, there is no aspect between Mercury and Mars at 21 Scorpio, the ruler of the 4th house. So however you look at it, the chart says they will not come to the games... and they didn't.

The following question had nothing to do with the person who asked it; it was just idle curiosity. He asked if the purchase by a local business man of the Bunker Hill mine in Kellogg, Idaho, would go through. The businessman had made a low bid for the defunct mine and it didn't look like he would get it.

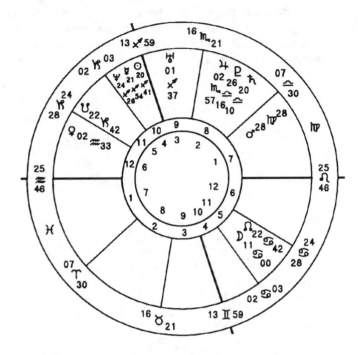

Example Chart #64:
12 Dec 1981 11:12 am PST Coeur d'Alene, ID 47N41 116W46
"Will Murchison get the Bunker Hill mine?"

The person inquired about is designated by the 7th house (renumber the chart), so the Sun at 20 Sagittarius rules him and is in his 4th. Mercury has recently passed the conjunction to the Sun, and is now at almost 22 Sagittarius, ruler of his 10th and applying to a conjunction of Neptune, co-ruler of the seller (because Pisces is intercepted in the buyer's 7th) at 24 Sagittarius, suggesting that a deal will be made. Venus, ruler of his 2nd (8th of the chart) at 2 Aquarius trines Saturn at 20 Libra, ruler of his investment 5th in his 2nd, indicating the potential for investment. The Moon, co-ruler of the question, at 11 Cancer quincunxes the Sun, Mercury and Neptune (collection and translation of light), further confirming the chance of the deal going through. But a quincunx suggests some kind of change or adjustment is necessary before things can proceed.

The union hierarchy in Pittsburgh would not honor the approval of the purchase by their membership and this event delayed the conclusion of the purchase until November 1, 1982. Unions are represented by Uranus at 1 Sagittarius which rules his 7th (open enemies) and is in his 3rd house of contracts and verbal negotiation. Uranus' sextile to Pluto at 26 Libra in the buyer's money house is very wide, but is applying. When we did this chart in class, we predicted that the sale would go through, but would take a while. We just didn't realize how long a while — nearly a year — it would be.

"CLASSIC" HORARY CHARTS

YES, I MAKE MISTAKES

We all have key charts which for one reason or another, open our eyes and really contribute to our learning. I refer to them as "classics." Here are some that helped me.

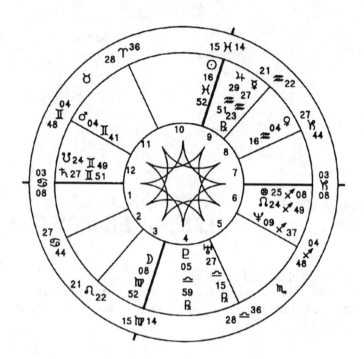

Example Chart #65:
7 March 1974 12:58 pm PDT Los Angeles, CA 34N04 118W15
"Where is my ring?"

An old school friend whom I hadn't seen in years had heard that I was an astrologer and wrote and asked me this question. I noted the time I read it and set up the chart for where I was.

The ring is represented by the ruler of the 2nd house, the Moon at 8 Virgo in the 3rd. The Part of Fortune in Sagittarius is in the 6th house. Both Virgo and the 6th house suggest containers, closets, hidden — not in plain view, possibly in a pocket. The Moon's rulership could indicate the kitchen as a possible place to look. Both the Part of Fortune in Sagittarius and its dispositor Jupiter in Aquarius as well as the Moon's dispositor, Mercury, in the 9th house denote a high area.

This was in my early days when I was not very experienced with Horary and overlooked some clues. I said she wouldn't find it because the Moon was below the horizon square Neptune and opposed the Sun. This information was based on ancient rules.

She called me two months later and asked why I didn't have the courage of my convictions. Her maid found the ring on a high shelf in the bedroom closet when she took her husband's shoes out to be shined.

Apparently the ring had been knocked off the bedside table into his shoe which was subsequently stored in the closet. They had gone on a cruise and when they returned, there was the ring. Technically, she didn't find it — the maid did. But I learned from this not to volunteer information that isn't asked for. All she had asked was where her ring was. I told her, but then added that I didn't think she would find it. I learned a lot from this Horary question. Don't volunteer information that isn't asked for.

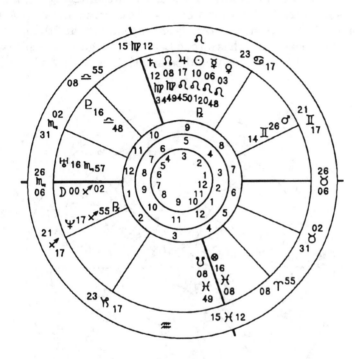

Example Chart #66:
2 Aug 1979 3:09 pm PDT Coeur d'Alene, ID 47N41 116W46
"Where are Jan's winter coats?"

My ex-daughter-in-law had moved to Coeur d'Alene and in moving into her new home had misplaced her winter coats. Although it was only August, she was concerned because she didn't want to have to replace them.

I really goofed on this chart. I used the 5th house to represent her, although I asked the question and called her by name. I should have turned the chart and used the 7th house for Jan, or at the very least looked for her in the 11th (of in-law children). In this chart the way I read it, the 6th house rules her possessions (2nd from 5th); Venus rules it and is in the 9th (5th from 5th) in Leo (child). Mercury also represents clothes and is in the 9th as well. I told her they were in a child's room or closet (*Pars Fortuna* in Pisces suggests an enclosed area), and that the child would find them or know where they were. She found her coats in her daughter's closet later that evening. Getting a correct answer with an incorrect approach was pure luck. This is why I suggest outlining your path logically before you even erect the chart for the Horary question.

Years later when I planned to use this chart for an article, I figured the answer "correctly." Fortunately I got the same answer. Mercury ruler of her 2nd (8th), since correctly she is found in the 7th house, is in Leo. Venus, ruler of her 5th is also in Leo, both suggesting a child would know where to look, or they would be in a child area of the house.

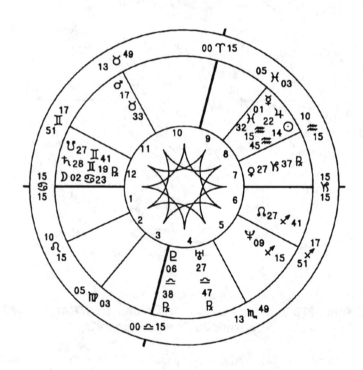

Example Chart #67:
3 Feb 1974 3:59 pm PDT Los Angeles, CA 34N04 118W15
"Will my house burn down by the end of this month?"

A friend had been reading her forecast in a pulp astrology magazine and it said to be careful of fire in the home. So she turned to her husband's sign forecast and it said essentially the same thing. She called me frantically and asked this question.

After I looked at the chart, I called and suggested that she come over and collaborate on the answer. The Moon ruled her and was in her 12th house at 2 Cancer square Pluto at 6 Libra in her 4th (home) which seemed very ominous to us; Venus, ruler of the 4th, is in the 7th at 27 Capricorn exactly square Uranus at 27 Libra in the 4th. We decided that her house would burn down and she purchased more fire insurance. Needless to say that when the house did not burn down, we were terribly disappointed. It was only after doing many more Horary charts that we learned that the squares in this chart were indicating "no" rather than "yes" answers.

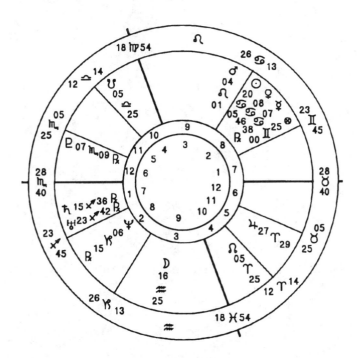

Example Chart #68:
12 Jul 1987 4:45 pm PDT Coeur d'Alene, ID 47W41 116W46
"Where are Rick's rings?"

This chart more than any other taught me the importance of identifying colors in helping to locate lost items. A client called and asked about her boyfriend's jewelry. He becomes the 7th house and his rings are ruled by Mercury (renumber the houses). Mercury is retrograde at 7 Cancer in his 2nd house indicating a.) he would get them back and b.) they were where he had put them. Since Mercury is in Cancer, the kitchen or bathroom are likely places, any place where there is plumbing. With the Part of Fortune at 25 Gemini disposited by Mercury, this concept is confirmed. It is possible they are near blue (Moon, ruler of Cancer in Aquarius), green (Cancer) and purple (Mercury conjunct Venus). See the color chart on page 84. They could also be where money is kept, in a jewel case or safe deposit box (all indicated by a 2nd house location).

Several months later when Rick's girlfriend called with a Horary question, I asked if he had ever found his rings and she said, "The rings were right where you told me... under the kitchen sink in a glass near a bottle of Windex (blue), a green sponge and a can of purple paint."

LESSON XVII

SOME QUESTIONS FOR YOU TO ANSWER

NOW THE READER GOES TO WORK

The following charts are for you to practice using the Horary Astrology rules given in this book. The answers are in the Appendix, but don't look at them until you try to figure these answers out. You may not reason the same way that I do, but if you get to the proper answer, it doesn't matter what route you take. However, be sure to write down your approach before you jump into the chart.

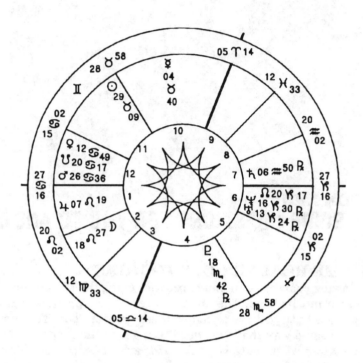

Test Chart #1:
20 May 1991 9:15 am PDT Coeur d'Alene, ID 47N41 116W46
"Should I build the houses for and with Garrick?"

A local contractor called with this question. A competitor had asked him to cooperate on the building of a small tract of houses and he was having difficulty making up his mind.

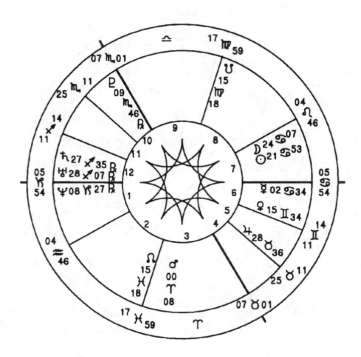

Test Chart #2:
13 Jul 1988 7:37 pm PDT Coeur d'Alene, ID 47N41 116W46
"Will Jerry get out on bail?"

A young man had been arrested on death threats and harassment charges and his mother asked the question.

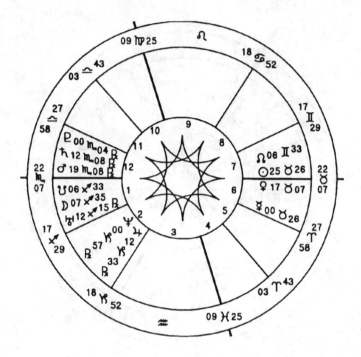

Test Chart #3:
15 May 1984 7:55 pm PDT Coeur d'Alene, ID 47N41 116W46
"Am I going to lose my home?"

A young woman who was recently divorced and had lost her job asked this question, because she was falling behind with her house payments.

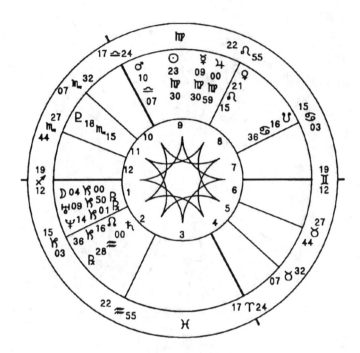

Test Chart #4:
16 Sep 1991 2:10 pm PDT Coeur d'Alene, ID 47N41 116W46
"Will Pete get his truck back?"

Several cars on one street had been stolen. My client's husband's truck was among them.

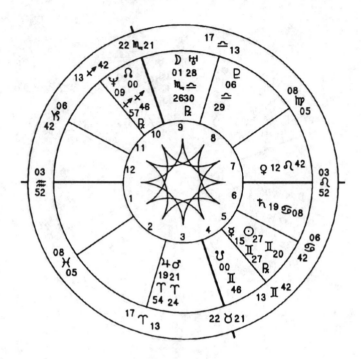

Test Chart #5:
18 Jun 1975 10:27 pm PDT Canoga Park, CA 34N12 118W38
"Is Matt guilty of the hit-and-run accident?"

A student called and said her boyfriend had been arrested for hit and run (two people were killed) and she wanted to know if he had done it.

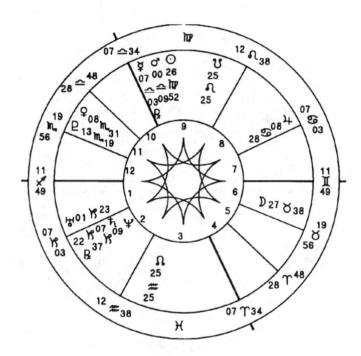

Test Chart #6:
19 Sep 1989 1:20 pm PDT Coeur d'Alene, ID 47N41 116W46
"Will the insurance company sue me? If so, will they win?"

The client had some trouble with her house flooding when a neighbor removed a retaining wall. Her insurance company had paid for repairs and much later she received a check from the neighbor for reimbursement. Several months later someone remarked that her insurance company could sue her to collect for the damage amount since she was paid twice, both by them and by the neighbor. How would you answer this question?

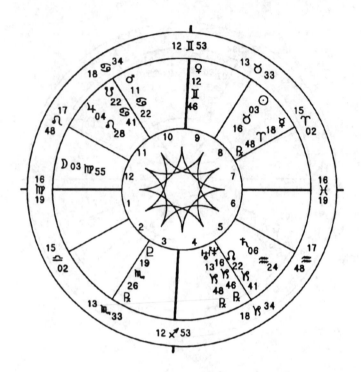

Test Chart #7:
23 April 1991 3:27 pm PDT Coeur d'Alene, ID 47N41 116W46
"Will my daughter-in-law be involved in a lawsuit?"

The woman's daughter-in-law worked at a school that was being sued by some parents and she was very concerned that she would have to testify.

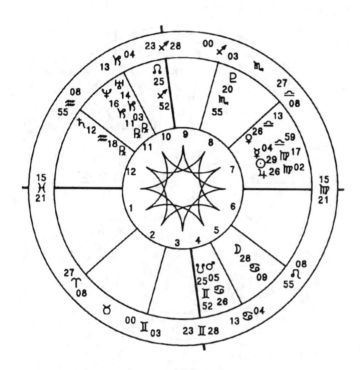

Test Chart #8:
21 Sep 1992 6:14 pm PDT Coeur d'Alene, ID 47N41 116W46
"Should I hire Gretel?"

A real estate agent had been looking for an assistant and a colleague recommended Gretel. They went to lunch together and the agent hired her. When she returned to her office and told her co-workers who she had hired, several of them said she had made a mistake, citing various reasons. When she got home, somewhat after the fact, she called and asked this question. How would you answer it?

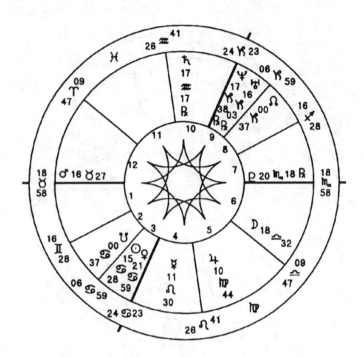

Test Chart #9:
7 Jul 1992 1:30 am PDT Coeur d'Alene, ID 47N41 116W46
"Should we buy the Osburn property?"

A friend called with this question. She is an astrologer and the question occurred to her at a strange time, but she requested that the chart be done for that time. It is rare to have the Sun in the first quadrant as the average person doesn't ask questions at the hours represented by those houses. This lady was considering buying a piece of property for her daughter and son-in-law in a neighboring town.

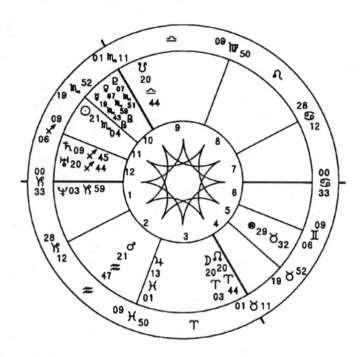

Test Chart #10:
13 Nov 1986 10:13 am PST Coeur d'Alene, ID 47N41 116W46
"Where is the headache medicine?"

A young mother had misplaced some strong headache medication and she was afraid her young toddler would find it before she did.

ELECTIONAL ASTROLOGY
BY MARION D. MARCH

H R

WHAT IS IT?

The name **Electional Astrology** actually states exactly what it is and what it can do. You **elect** or choose a moment in time to erect a chart for a specific purpose. Nicholas Devore in his *Encyclopedia of Astrology* states: "It is a method by which you choose a suitable time for commencing any honestly conceived and reasonable project or endeavor."

You elect or choose to get married, move, buy a house, take a new job, start a new business, go on a trip, file a lawsuit, draw up a will, or any other important matter you decide on.

Actually, the theory of **electing** a special moment in time is the reverse technique of Horary where a moment in time is used to ask a question seeking an answer. **Electional Astrology** knows the answer it wants and is looking for the suitable time to attain it. Both Horary and Electional Astrology have their roots in ancient times and some of these methodologies can be traced as far back as 500 BC, the time of Pythagoras, who provided the mathematical theories necessary to calculate and interpret that type of horoscope.

The Transcendentals — New Applications Of Old Techniques

Before you actually work with a method you should understand why it is where it is today. Though the old "tried and true" way worked, time marches on and with it comes change. In this time of atomic energy, we need the planet Pluto and cannot be satisfied with Mars alone. Since astrology is a symbolic language, each astrologer has to find her/his own solution to how Pluto is best used. Some will give Pluto the total rulership of Scorpio; others will say that it is the main ruler with Mars as the subruler and still others prefer to use both planets as co-rulers.

The same, of course, applies to Uranus and Neptune, neither having been discovered until the 18th and 19th century respectively, one now ruling Aquarius, the other Pisces in this modern day and age, while Saturn and Jupiter were considered to be the old, classical rulers of these signs.

I use Uranus as the sole ruler of Aquarius and Neptune as uniquely being in charge of Pisces, while I permit Mars a slight ownership of Scorpio. There are many considerations that led me to this usage of the transcendentals.

1. **In years past, before the discovery of the outer planets, astrologers differentiated between planets of day versus planets of night.** The positive signs were always assigned the **day home**, while the negative signs became the **night home**; thus, Saturn ruled Aquarius by day and Capricorn at night. Jupiter's day home was Sagittarius, while it reigned over Pisces at night. Mars' realm of day was Aries, that of night, Scorpio.

Unfortunately, terms such as positive/negative (Joan and I call them active/passive) as well as day/night, in today's language usage invoke visions of good and bad, light and dark, black and white. In the eye of the beholder Aquarius can be considered good (positive/day), while poor Capricorn may end up as the bad guy/gal with the black hat (negative/ dark)!

2. As I realized this, I understood that **not only do our languages differ, but so do our ways of life, our whole world.** Planets seem to be discovered when something so radical happens on earth that the old interpretations simply do not suffice. Uranus' discovery in 1781 took place at the time of the Industrial Revolution and the harnessing of electricity...both momentous events that would be hard to explain and difficult to incorporate under the aegis of Saturn/Aquarius.

Neptune's discovery in 1846 heralded the birth of psychoanalysis, a totally new approach to life that encouraged us to look within, into our deep, subconscious 12th house Piscean nature. All of sudden Jupiter's idealistic and optimistic nature did not suffice for Pisces.

Last but not least, Pluto was discovered in 1930 at the dawning of the Atomic Age, a totally plutonic event for which the element plutonium is needed in order to provide the necessary chain reaction. How can energetic, hardworking, aggressive, yet up-front, open, "what you see is what you get" Mars ever fulfill the hidden needs and depth we attribute to Pluto?

3. **Uranus has now been around for over 200 years and we have had ample opportunity to see how it works,** enough to convince me that the planet Uranus and the sign Aquarius work in many similar

fashions, that they are a near perfect blend and that in this century, Uranus is much more representative of Aquarian matters than Saturn.

Astrologers have been observing Neptune for nearly 150 years. To my way of thinking this planet is much more compatible with the sign Pisces than outgoing, hopeful, ever proselytizing and not always sensitive Jupiter.

4. Since I have not been here for 200 or 150 years, am a skeptic at heart and like to be sure before I adopt any rule, in the late '70s, I spent two years using Saturn as well as Uranus as ruler of Aquarius in all my chart interpretations, in comparison/composites and especially in electional work where some old time astrologers claim that the "old" rules work much better than the new ones. Since that little experiment, **I am totally convinced that in today's world Uranus rules Aquarius and Neptune rules Pisces and that we don't need Saturn or Jupiter as co- or subrulers.**

5. Why can't I be as sure about Pluto? First of all, it has only been in our consciousness since 1930 — a mere 60-plus years. Its orbit is so eccentric that at times its trajectory is inside that of Neptune. Does its significance change when it is not the furthest planet from Earth? We have not observed Pluto long enough to know. Many of our considerations stem from examining not only electional, but also natal charts, yet Pluto's motion is so slow that timing is hard to gauge. More often than not it seems to sow the seed while some other, faster moving planet, frequently Mars, has to come along and trigger the Pluto contact before we take action.

For all these reasons, I still use Mars as the subruler for Scorpio, mainly when doing mundane work, electionals and horaries, all areas where the free will has little chance to express. When delineating a natal chart, I still add Mars' position to any physical descriptions for those who have Scorpio rising.

Electional Versus Natal Charts

In today's astrological world psychological insights and terms, particularly Jungian ones, have become totally accepted. Very few astrologers, when updating a horoscope, will tell a client that divorce is imminent... instead they may ask about the marriage and warn that it is time to talk to each other, see a family therapist or some such thing, else there may be a danger of misunderstandings leading to possible separation or divorce. In other words, the problem is the client's to solve. S/he of her/his free will can decide which course of action to take. The planets will not bring on a divorce, nor can they stop one, but their activity can help clients identify problems and give guidance as to when to act.

An electional chart comes from a totally different perspective. A client asks you to find the best possible moment to, for example, send a book to be published. There is no psychology here, no feelings to get hurt, no feathers to ruffle, only a practical effort to enable the client to be successful. Therefore, many of the old rules apply. What you see is what you get. No embellishments, no toning down of statements. If you choose this day or this hour, these are the probable results. The ruler of the 9th house (publishing) trine the ruler of the Ascendant (client) is a good indicator for success. If, however, they square or oppose each other, let's pick another time. To a certain degree there still is free will, because the client has the final word as to which possible chart to use, or, for that matter, not to take any action.

Many astrologers follow the old rules so completely that they see Mars, Saturn, Uranus, Neptune and Pluto as malefic in every sense of the word. Again, you, the astrologer will have to be the final arbiter, but for myself I cannot accept any planet as being bad or good. I think they all have negative and positive attributes, so I'm very careful into which house certain planets fall. I may not like Saturn in the 9th where it may deter me in my ability to convince the publisher that my book is just what he wants...but I may love to place it in the 6th house where it will help me to concentrate, to work hard, to be disciplined.

The Philosophy Of Electional Astrology

There are myriad reasons to calculate an electional chart and find the perfect time to start something. Just be sure that "something" is truly meaningful; don't, even for learning purposes, playfully erect a chart for washing your bed sheets or having breakfast. What you learn will be misleading. Rather go back to moments in your life that were successful beginnings of some momentous happening... when you started your first job, got married, moved into a new area or house. Astrology, including Electional and Horary, is not a parlor game, and if you wish it to be helpful, you have to treat it seriously.

finish

H R to ---?

GENERAL RULES FOR ELECTIONAL CHARTS

In order to do anything well, you must first understand the rules. Though astrology is astrology is astrology...there are definite guidelines you need, especially since Electional Astrology requires some procedures not used when dealing with natal charts, progressions, directions, transits, synastry or other types of astrology. After you have digested the general rules, you will learn the specifics as they relate to the various subjects applicable to this type of astrology.

1. **Use applying aspects only.** By the time the aspects separate, the elected event may be over. Orbs *per se* do not exist in Electional Astrology. As long as an aspect is applying, it does not matter whether it is 0° or 29° in orb. An aspect continues until either planet leaves the sign it is in. Orbs only play a role in timing (which is discussed in Lessons V, VI and VII).

2. **Use the so-called "classical" aspects: conjunction, sextile, square, trine and opposition.** The quincunx (inconjunct), so important in natal interpretation because of its psychological application, seems to have much less import in Electional Astrology.

3. **The Moon is the primary consideration in electional charts.** It is the fastest moving of the ten planets and is often used as a timer. A difficult Moon precludes ease in accomplishing the specific happening you elect to do.

   a) Therefore, **avoid squares from the Moon.** Oppositions are less troublesome than squares, as are quincunxes, though the first can signify antagonism from someone and the latter suggests delays as well as the need for some change or reorganization.

   b) **A waxing Moon (a time of growth) is usually considered more advantageous than a waning one,** but stay away from an exact New Moon...wait at least 12 hours until the Moon is noticeably increasing in light.

c) **A Void-of-Course Moon rarely brings the desired result** in electional charts unless you are opting for a nonoccurrence, such as mailing your income tax so it will NOT be audited.

d) Most astrological calendars have daily **lunar aspects**, thus making your life relatively easy.

4. Except for Saturn-ruled affairs (building, architecture, administration, etc.) **try to keep Saturn out of the angles.** Cadent houses are best, though Saturn in the 12th should be avoided if possible when buying houses or land or in any similar situation where you don't want a covert situation revealed after you have bought the object in question.

5. It is also better to **keep Uranus and, under certain circumstances, Mars out of the angles.**

6. **Choose a Rising Sign that supports the matter you are electing.** For example: Gemini, Virgo or Sagittarius for the publication of a book.

7. **Most electional charts benefit by having the Sun, Moon, Venus and Jupiter above the horizon.**

8. I rarely use the Lunar Nodes in Electional Astrology, but according to the old rules, the **North Node** is considered fortunate and even lucky, but the **South Node** is deemed unfavorable.

9. **Cardinal Signs** are best for new ventures and events that require initiative and energy. **Fixed Signs** have a lasting quality, though at times it may take longer to get results. **Mutable Signs** are flexible.

10. **Remember the nature of the planets which can describe the areas they are best suited to.**

a) If you want to sell your car, place **Mercury** in a prominent position.

b) Artistic pursuits should favor a strongly placed **Venus.**

c) If you wish to start a strenuous exercise program, place **Mars** in an angle.

d) Travel benefits from **Jupiter** in high focus.

e) A strong **Saturn** is necessary for most businesses, since it embodies discipline and organization.

f) A well-placed **Uranus** is superb for unique ventures as well as those which involve inventions, computers, novelties or gadgetry.

g) A 1st or 10th house **Neptune** may be well-suited for the film industry, to initiate a movie, write the script, direct or produce, or other areas where charisma, glamour or creativity are important; as well as endeavors involving shipping or oil — but Neptune can be misleading in these houses in other matters.

h) The intensity of **Pluto** needs to be handled with care, but it can be very beneficial in realms where power plays are called for.

11. Despite some astrologers' predictions of doom and gloom regarding **interceptions and retrogrades** in horoscopes, I have never found either to really hurt or hinder anything or anyone in a natal chart. At times an intercepted or retrograde planet may slow the action or indicate that you should look before you leap, but in no way do I consider this detrimental. I approach Electional charts with a similar attitude and have not found intercepted signs to be weak or nonfunctioning as some old books expect you to believe. I have also discovered that a retrograde planet does not seem to hold back or negate the election, unless it rules the Ascendant or the house pertaining to the main subject of the election (10th for business, 7th for marriage, etc.).

a) If you must choose an optimum time to sue someone, it is best not to have Jupiter retrograde ruling the 9th or 7th houses. A retrograde Jupiter cannot always be avoided since it is retrograde for nearly four months each year, but you can circumvent having it rule the legal houses or the Ascendant which rules you.

b) I try to stay away from **Mercury retrograde** periods any time I have to sign a contract or buy a car, not just in an electional chart, but on general principles. Mercury is never retrograde for more than 24 days, so it is, under most circumstances, a reasonable time to wait. If the elected event cannot be postponed, keep Mercury-ruled signs away from the Ascendant and those houses directly affected by the election.

c) Venus retrograde is not advisable for wedding charts (Venus = love and partnership) or buying expensive items (Venus = value).

12. After doing literally hundreds of horoscopes, I have realized that many of the old restrictions do not seem to apply anymore. Therefore, I will not even mention them in this book. However, **one which needs to be watched carefully is if the last aspect of the Moon is voided because the planet it aspects changes signs before the Moon reaches that point.** Example: The Moon at 14 Taurus must trine Mercury at 29 Capricorn before it enters 0 Aquarius. Yet by the time the Moon reaches 29 Capricorn (30 hours, more or less), Mercury may have moved into Aquarius and thus deny the Moon the trine aspect. This situation has often proven to withhold the expected result of the election, so be sure to carefully check planets which may have moved into a new sign.

13. Challenged planets can be strengthened by placing them in flowing aspect with the angles or the rulers of the angles; or, according to the ancients, with the Part of Fortune. Example: Mars square the Sun and quincunx Mercury, but trine the Ascendant or Ascendant ruler.

If your astrological knowledge is weak in the areas relating to each planet and house, refer to Rex Bills' *Rulership Book* or Michael Munkasey's *Astrological Thesaurus, Book I*, or for a classical interpretation, *The Book of Rulerships* by Dr. J. Lee Lehman.

An Electional chart is the Birth Chart for whatever event you choose...a wedding, a business opening, buying or selling a home. Therefore, it should reflect and benefit the event and it is the primary chart you deal with. Your natal horoscope, or that of your client, is secondary in importance. You should look for favorable aspects between the Electional chart and the natal chart only after you have fulfilled as many of the electional rules as possible.

Of course your natal chart will indicate significant events by progression, direction or transits, such as your wish to marry, open a new business, move or whatever the case may be.

In this book I will teach you the Electional rules for the most often asked occasions, namely **marriage, moving into a house, buying or selling a house, buying a new car, starting a new business venture, taking a trip, lawsuits,** what can and cannot be done in case of **surgery** and helpful hints for the new childbearing sciences such as *in vitro* or artificial insemination. **Most important: there is no perfect chart.** You will always have to make some concessions along the way.

LESSON III

MARRIAGE

TYING THE KNOT

One of the most frequent Electional requests I receive is: "Please find me a good day and time to get married." To save untold hours of work, I ask my clients for certain parameters, such as a definite month, better yet the weekends in that month, and best of all just one or two possible dates. With too much leeway, the responsibility for the astrologer is awesome and the time needed is more than most clients can afford.

Remember: A perfect chart is impossible to calculate for any Election...marriage, a new business or anything at all!

Marriage Rules

When calculating the time, remember: **the marriage starts with the first "I do!"**

1. There should be **no squares from the Moon** and it should **not be Void of Course.**

A **waxing Moon** (between New and Full) **is better** than a waning one (between Full and New).

2. **Fixed signs rising** are best when you want a long lasting relationship. Next are the **Cardinal** signs, especially **Libra** (relationship oriented), **Capricorn** (the need for any venture to be successful) and **Cancer** (nurturing). Aries and Mutable signs can indicate very short lived situations.

3. Try to have **the Sun and Moon in harmonious aspect** to each other because they represent the groom and the bride.

4. A relationship usually works well when the **ruler of the Ascendant (1st) and Descendant (7th)** are in **harmonious aspect** to each other since they represent the two parties in question.

5. Because **Saturn** can limit or bring on delays, it should not be placed in an Angular house. It fares best in **Cadent** (3rd, 6th, 9th, 12th) houses or, if that is not possible, put it in one of the Succedent (2nd, 5th, 8th, 11th) houses. If possible avoid all applying aspects to Saturn, including conjunctions. When these aspects become exact, there could be misunderstandings, feelings of neglect or sadness of some kind.

6. If you want the relationship to proceed in a pleasant fashion, and you wouldn't be setting up an Electional chart if you didn't, **keep Uranus out of the Angular houses**, especially the 1st and 7th.

7. **The luminaries (Sun and Moon), as well as Venus and Jupiter** (the benefics) **should be above the horizon**, if possible. Three out of four is good. Elevated planets are more noticeable and seem to bring a certain ease to the elected venture.

8. Try to have **Venus** (woman) **and Mars** (man) **in harmonious aspect** to each other, also **Venus** (love and partnership) and the **Ascendant/Descendant** (the couple), **Jupiter** (luck and growth) and the **Ascendant/Descendant**, and the **Moon** (feelings) and **Venus** (harmony). In other words, **a strong, well-aspected Venus** is very beneficial.

9. **Avoid the Moon in Scorpio** where it is in its fall and where it can be secretive and possessive, not exactly conducive to a happy relationship. A **Libra Moon**, on the other hand, works quite well in a marriage Electional chart since it seeks harmony and balance. Strong and well-matched couples seem to do well with the **Moon in Leo**.

10. **The Sun or Moon approaching a square or opposition to Uranus may indicate a separation** or divorce when the aspect becomes exact.

11. **A retrograde Venus is not advised** for any marriage chart. Since Venus only retrogrades for about 40 days every two years, it is fairly easy to avoid.

These are some of the important rules for marriage Elections. What follows are charts from my files...actual examples to teach you how to implement the foregoing directives.

Tools of the Trade

To simplify matters when you undertake Electional charting, it is very helpful to have an astrological calendar which indicates the daily aspects made by the Moon. (See sample pages on pages 142 and 143.) Most of the above events will have better results if you "elect" a day where the Moon makes no squares before it leaves the sign of the zodiac it is in. This automatically eliminates quite a few days to plan events. Many astrologers with a large electional clientele go through the entire calendar and put a green check mark on the so-called "good" days or code the "bad" ones with a red X.

It is also very convenient to have a computer with an astrological program. I remember so well the old days (BC — before computers) when I sat and calculated for hours what now takes mere minutes. My software (Pathfinder) has a great feature called "Elections" where, by pressing just one key, I can change the year, month, day, hour or minute... a most useful feature.

A Marriage Example

A client named Lis called. She and Jim wanted to get married in June, 1992, preferably Saturday, June 6th or Sunday, June 7th; June 13th or 14th would also be acceptable. They both worked and had only limited vacation time and wished to get married in the Los Angeles area where most of their family members lived. Thus, my Electional charts were calculated for Pacific Daylight Time.

Step 1: Referring to my astrological calendar for June 1992, I noted that on June 6th, the Moon was in Virgo and did not enter Libra until Monday, June 8th at 11:33 am PDT. Unfortunately it squared Venus and the Sun before it left Virgo and these squares should certainly be avoided in a marriage chart.

Even June 7th was risky since the Moon squared Mercury on June 8th before it left Virgo. This is probably the least difficult square, one that I might use on occasion. But first I checked the next possible dates, June 13th and 14th. The Moon was in Sagittarius; not only was there a full Moon, a Lunar Eclipse (Sun opposed the Moon), but before it left the sign, it also opposed Venus. None of this suggested that it was an auspicious time to be married.

Step 2: None of the proposed dates looked promising, but under the circumstances, I tried some charts for Sunday, June 7th, after 1:47 pm (Sun square the Moon) and, if possible, before 3:34 pm to take advantage of the Moon/Neptune trine.

69

WEDNESDAY 3	Eastern	Pacific
	☽ in ♋	☽ in ♋
	☽ v/c 8:31p	☽ v/c 5:31p
	☽☍♅ 12:37p	☽☍♅ 9:37a
	☽☍♆ 2:32p	☽☍♆ 11:32a
Leo Gorcey 1915	☽△♇ 6:38p	☽△♇ 3:38p
Jefferson Davis 1808	☽□♂ 8:31p	☽□♂ 5:31p

THURSDAY 4	Eastern	Pacific
	☽→♌ 9:35a	☽→♌ 6:35a
Sandra Haynie 1943		
Andrea Jaeger 1965	☿△♄ 3:50a	☿△♄ 0:50a

FRIDAY 5	Eastern	Pacific
	☽ in ♌	☽ in ♌
		☽ v/c 9:57p
		☽✱♀ 3:43a
	☽✱♀ 6:43a	☽✱☉ 7:42a
	☽✱☉ 10:42a	☽☍♄ 1:08p
	☽☍♄ 4:08p	☽□♇ 5:14p
Ken Follett 1949	☽□♇ 8:14p	☽✱☿ 7:35p
Tommie Smith 1944	☽✱☿ 10:35p	☽△♂ 9:57p

SATURDAY 6	Eastern	Pacific
	☽ v/c 0:57a	☽→♍ 8:28a
	☽→♍ 11:28a	
	☽△♂ 0:57a	
Willie Davenport 1943	☿✱♂ 9:48p	☿✱♂ 6:48p
Bjorn Borg 1956	☽☌♃ 10:40p	☽☌♃ 7:40p

Daylight Saving Time

Reproduced by permission of Quicksilver Productions.

JUNE 1992

S	M	T	W	T	F	S
	1	2	3	4	5	6
7	8	9	10	11	12	13
14	15	16	17	18	19	20
21	22	23	24	25	26	27
28	29	30				

MAY 1992

S	M	T	W	T	F	S
					1	2
3	4	5	6	7	8	9
10	11	12	13	14	15	16
17	18	19	20	21	22	23
24/31	25	26	27	28	29	30

JULY 1992

S	M	T	W	T	F	S
			1	2	3	4
5	6	7	8	9	10	11
12	13	14	15	16	17	18
19	20	21	22	23	24	25
26	27	28	29	30	31	

GEMINI ♊

SUNDAY 7

Eastern	Pacific
First Quarter 17♍20 4:47p	First Quarter 17♍20 1:47p
☽ in ♍	☽ in ♍
☽□♀ 1:49p	☽□♀ 10:49a
☽△♅ 4:31p	☽△♅ 1:31p
☽□☉ 4:47p	☽□☉ 1:47p
☽△♆ 6:34p	☽△♆ 3:34p
☽✶♇ 10:48p	☽✶♇ 7:48p

Shavuot
Whit Sunday, Pentecost
Prince (Nelson Rogers) 1958

MONDAY 8

Eastern	Pacific
☽ v/c 10:22a	☽ v/c 7:22a
☽→♎ 2:33p	☽→♎ 11:33a
☽□☿ 10:22a	☽□☿ 7:22a
☉△♄ 7:14p	☉△♄ 4:14p

Don Grady 1944
LeRoy Neiman 1926

TUESDAY 9

Eastern	Pacific
☽ in ♎	☽ in ♎
	☿→♋ 11:27a
☿→♋ 2:27p	♀△♄ 5:00p
♀△♄ 8:00p	☽□♅ 5:27p
☽□♅ 8:27p	☽□♆ 7:38p
☽□♆ 10:38p	☽△♄ 7:41p
☽△♄ 10:41p	☽△♀ 7:57p
☽△♀ 10:57p	☽△☉ 9:49p

George Axelrod 1922
Les Paul 1916

Reproduced by permission of Quicksilver Productions.

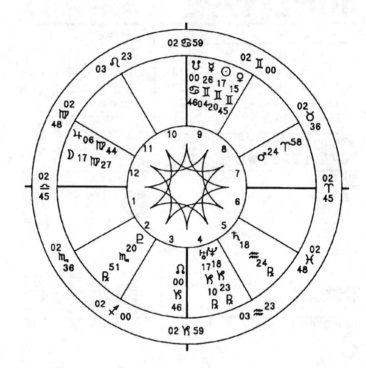

Example Chart #1:
7 June 1992 2:00 pm PDT Los Angeles, CA 34N03 118W15
Possible Wedding chart for Lis and Jim.

I noted that the Moon was past the square to the Sun (by seven minutes). This chart did not have a fixed Ascendant, but Libra rising is nice for a marriage. The Descendant ruler Venus at 15 Gemini sextiled the Ascendant ruler Mars at 25 Aries. Saturn was in the 5th house (succedent), but unfortunately Uranus and Neptune were angular (in the 4th) and even worse...Mars was in the 7th where it does not augur well for a one-on-one relationship.

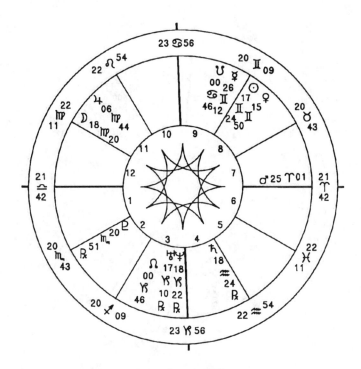

Example Chart #2:
7 Jun 1992 3:30 pm PDT Los Angeles, CA 34N03 118W15
Another proposed Wedding chart for Lis and Jim.

To move Mars out of the 7th into the 6th, it became necessary to advance the time approximately 90 minutes, since the cusp of the 7th was 2 Aries while Mars was at 25 Aries and the Ascendant/Descendant axis moves one degree more or less every four minutes. (22 × 4 = 88). When viewing Chart #2, note that Mars was still in the 7th house by four minutes and Saturn was now in the 4th, an unacceptable position.

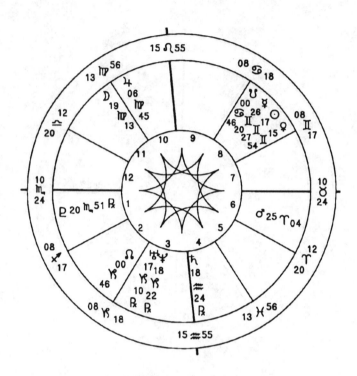

Example Chart #3:
7 June 1992 5:00 pm PDT Los Angeles, CA 34N03 118W15
A third proposed Wedding chart for Lis and Jim.

Advancing the time an hour and a half, Saturn was still in the 4th house, and even worse, Pluto was in the 1st. To move Pluto into the 12th house, the Ascendant must be past 20 Scorpio 52, or more than 10 degrees later. To be on the safe side, I set up the next chart for 6:00 pm, an hour later.

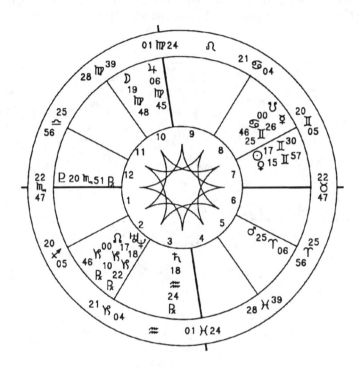

Example Chart #4:
7 Jun 1992 6:00 pm PDT Los Angeles, CA 34N03 118W15
A fourth proposed Wedding chart for Lis and Jim.

This Electional chart has potential. In checking the list of desirable positions:

There is a fixed Ascendant (Scorpio); the Sun and Moon do not aspect each other; the Descendant ruler Venus sextiles Ascendant subruler Mars and quincunxes Ascendant ruler Pluto. Saturn is in a cadent house as is Pluto and neither Neptune nor Uranus are angular. Both luminaries as well as Venus and Jupiter, are above the horizon. Unfortunately, in order to get the planets into the right houses, it was necessary to pass up the Moon's trine to Neptune, but we still have the approaching sextile to the Ascendant ruler Pluto, which is positive. But, and this is worth considering... the Moon's last aspect is a square to Mercury. Is there any way to avoid it?

Step 3: I checked Friday, June 5th on my calendar and observed that the Moon was in Leo, and if I calculated the chart for approximately 6:00 pm, the wheel was similar to the one on June 7th (#4), but the

Moon sextiled Mercury and trined Mars before it left Leo. In comparison to the previous charts, that sounded absolutely wonderful.

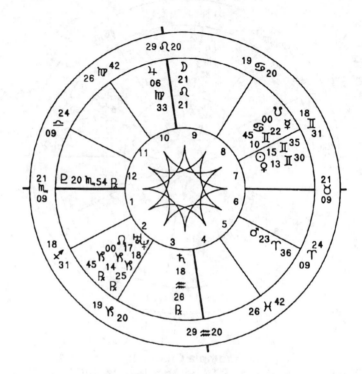

Example Chart #5:
5 Jun 1992 6:00 pm PDT Los Angeles, CA 34N03 118W15
Voila! The best possible Wedding chart for Lis and Jim.

This chart has all the planets in the right houses, a fixed Ascendant, good aspects from Venus to Mars, a harmonious Sun and Moon, and although the Moon has passed the sextile to the Sun, it will sextile Venus (ruler of the Descendant) and trine Mars (subruler of the Ascendant) before it leaves Leo.

I called Lis and asked if she could possibly consider Friday evening. I cited all the benefits; we discussed how a 5:30 pm invitation was quite feasible; how she could serve cocktails and dinner afterwards and, to make a long story short, they married on Friday, June 5th at 6:00PM.

More Wedding Chart Examples

The previous exercise gave some insight into the intricacies of finding the right time for an Electional chart. For further illumination, here are more marriage charts, some that have proven successful as well as other more recent ones where for one reason or another, the rules needed to be stretched.

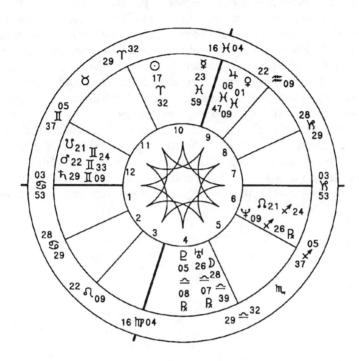

Example Chart #6:
7 Apr 1974 11:00 am PDT Sherman Oaks, CA 34N09 118W26
Wedding chart for Marianne and Fred.

This young couple did not give me very many dates to choose from, since she was a 21-year-old student on her Easter break and he had just started a new job and did not want to take more than one day off. On the day picked, the Moon was in Libra (a good marriage Moon) and makes only one aspect, a trine to Saturn, but that is the key to this chart. The Moon rules the Cancer Ascendant and the Capricorn Descendant is ruled by Saturn in a cadent house and the trine indicates that the energy between bride and groom flows easily. The Sun, Venus and Jupiter are above the horizon. Venus (ruler of the 5th house of love and children) is quite strong in this chart...exalted in Pisces and conjunct Jupiter which is dignified in the house it rules, the 9th. Both planets trine the Ascendant and sextile the Descendant. These placements represent the positive rules that were followed.

What about some of the problem areas? Uranus is angular (4th) receiving an eight and a half degree opposition from the 10th house Sun. This measurement equates to about eight and a half years. This couple did not divorce as could have occurred with the Sun/Uranus opposition; in fact they are still happily married. However, they have moved seven times in 18 years of marriage (Uranus in the 4th); not only from city to city, but from country to country, and he has had four major job changes. When the Sun/Uranus opposition became exact, they bought their first house and took on a huge mortgage.

As stated previously, it is impossible to find a perfect chart, thus in many cases you will have to make concessions. Since the man in this case has an Aquarius Sun and the woman an Aquarian Moon, this couple has learned how to handle Uranus. I figured that of all the possible difficulties, this might be one they could best overcome. They have.

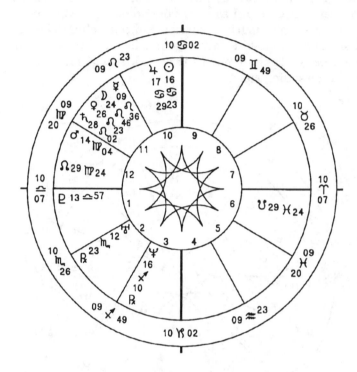

Example Chart #7:
8 Jul 1978 12:15 pm AHST Wailua, HI 22N03 159W20
Wedding chart for Jan and Rob.

This couple wanted to get married in Hawaii in the famous Fern Grotto and the only day, or for that matter, time available was July 8th at noon. The ceremony usually takes 15 minutes. When Jan, my client, asked me to look at the wedding chart, I was quite disturbed and begged her to have a private wedding, just the bride and groom, some time before and then have the lovely ceremony on July 8th. She did not want to do that.

Can you see what worried me in this chart? The Moon makes only two aspects, a fortunate conjunction to Venus, followed by a conjunction to Saturn in three and a quarter degrees. Chart ruler Venus made only the conjunction to Saturn. Pluto on the 1st house can be very intense, a bit too much so for Jan and Rob in my estimation.

They said their "I do's" at 12:15 pm on the day in question. After two years the marriage started going downhill. Jan met a dashing young man at work, fell in love and in October 1981 got a divorce (three years and three months to the day after the wedding). What saddened me was the fact that though I saw possible problems, I could not prevent the break-up, despite much discussion and counseling. The good news is that she and her dashing lover married in 1982, are very happy and their cute baby daughter makes three. This time she gave me more choices for a wedding chart.

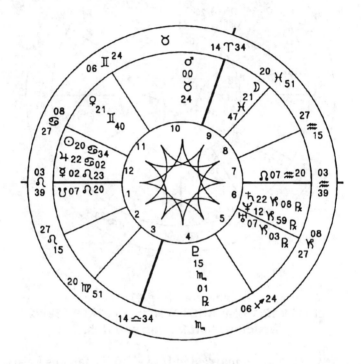

Example Chart #8:
13 Jul 1990 7:00 am MEST Basel, SWTZ 47N33 7E35
Wedding chart for Franca and Carl.

In 1990, I faced a rather interesting problem. A 51-year-old long-time client, very anxious to marry and have children, after many long- and short-term affairs, finally fell in love with a 27-year-old Swiss scientist whom he met while attending a seminar in Basel, Switzerland. We had very few options on the day, just the time. In other words, the Sun/Saturn opposition could not be avoided. Therefore, it was necessary to choose a good house position. I calculated some 20 charts, just to satisfy myself that nothing better was around the corner. Since my client wanted children, it became expedient to look not only for the usual marital guidelines, but also to fortify the 5th house. In Switzerland in the middle of

July the only possible fixed signs on the Ascendant are Leo or Scorpio. By the time Scorpio rises, the Moon is void of course. Leo rising is better for this marriage chart, since my client has a Leo Sun and the bride-to-be has Leo on the 7th cusp.

The next problem to overcome was the Moon/Venus square, yet still be in time for the lunar trine to Jupiter and sextile to Saturn. As you can see, finding an optimum time for an Electional chart becomes a juggling act!

In this chart the Moon is in Pisces in the 9th house, past the square to Venus, trine Jupiter and sextile Saturn. The Ascendant is fixed; its ruler, the Sun, will conjunct Jupiter which rules the 5th house of children. The Aquarius Descendant is ruled by Uranus in the 5th. The Sun is past the opposition, but as observed earlier is opposing Saturn, an aspect to be avoided...but a) my client chose this day and b) it really describes the age difference between them (Moon/Saturn would have done the same). The Sun, Moon, Venus and Jupiter are all above the horizon. Since we know there is no perfect chart, where are the problems in this one?

Pluto and Mars are angular and Pluto rules the interception in the 4th house. Both my client and his bride are strong individuals and although she is much younger, I wonder if she'll assert herself and if power struggles might ensue. Mars is in and rules the 10th house and this could indicate clashes regarding "my" career versus "your" career.

It's too early to know, but so far, so good. They seem very happy after three and a half years of marriage and have two little boys and a girl.

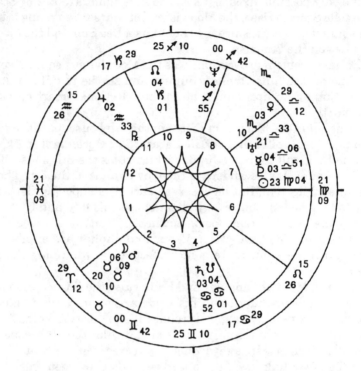

Example Chart #9:
15 Sep 1973 7:00 pm PDT Tahoe City, NV 39N10 120W09
Proposed Wedding chart for Chris and Brett.

A young couple were planning a wedding at Lake Tahoe with a few friends in attendance. They had selected Saturday evening at 7 pm for the ceremony.

Pisces rising is not especially recommended for marriage charts because of its mutability and dreamlike or illusory qualities. Although the Ascendant/Descendant rulers (Mercury and Neptune) were sextile, the Moon applied to a conjunction to Mars in the 2nd house which promised possible arguments and disagreements over money matters. Saturn in the 4th and Uranus in the 7th were worrisome to say the least. I asked if they would consider putting off the actual ceremony until afternoon of the next day. They agreed. From the conversation, I understood that they would like to work together. Here is the wedding chart I came up with:

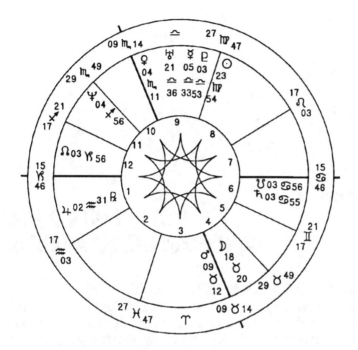

Example Chart #10:
16 Sep 1973 3:45 pm PDT Tahoe City, CA 39N10 120W09
The actual Wedding chart for Chris and Brett.

The Moon has passed the conjunction to Mars, but will still trine the Sun. Saturn, the Ascendant ruler, is out of the 4th and has moved into the 6th house of work. Uranus and Pluto are out of the angles. The Sun and Venus are still above the horizon. Though natal charts are secondary in importance when doing Electionals, it is worth noting that the bride has Capricorn rising while the groom has a Cancer Ascendant. This chart really reflects the couple in every way. They are still married, are successful business entrepreneurs working together, and they have four charming children.

LESSON IV

MOVING INTO A HOUSE, CONDOMINIUM OR APARTMENT

WHERE YOU HANG YOUR HAT

This is another frequent request for an Electional chart, which is not surprising in the United States where people move on an average of once every seven years. It does not really matter if the place you move into is rented, owned or loaned, if it is a house, an apartment or just a room... as long as it is going to be your abode, where you hang your proverbial hat for a certain amount of time, it is considered **home**.

When calculating the time, **moving in starts when the first personal object is moved into the home.**

1. Most of the general rules (see page 135) apply, with the Moon again being the primary consideration. Therefore, **avoid squares, be careful with oppositions and quincunxes** and, of course, **shun a Void-of-Course Moon.**

2. Your astrological knowledge and good common sense will help you determine most other factors. Since your new home is to be pleasant and free from trouble, be sure the **ruler of the Ascendant** (you) is **in positive aspect** (trine, sextile, conjunction) to the **ruler of the 4th house** (the home).

3. Unless this is a temporary residence, or for some reason you don't wish to stay in the home for any length of time, try for a **fixed Ascendant** (Taurus, Leo, Scorpio, Aquarius).

4. **Avoid Saturn and Mars in angular houses,** and unless you thrive on excitement, keep **Uranus** away as well. For all three of these planets, cadent houses are best. An astrologer friend planned a move and

totally overlooked the transcendentals. His electional chart for the move had Uranus in the 4th house. The first night in the new house, he blew a fuse when he hooked up the hi-fi. A week later sparks flew out of his iron and burned his arm. A month later, during a thunderstorm, lightning hit the power line next door and he was without power for two days.

5. **Elevated luminaries** (Sun and Moon) and so-called **benefics** (Venus and Jupiter) are helpful.

6. Though you should not **buy** a house while **Mercury** or **Venus** are **retrograde**, it does not seem to affect the time you move into the place. Since practice makes perfect, here are a few actual cases.

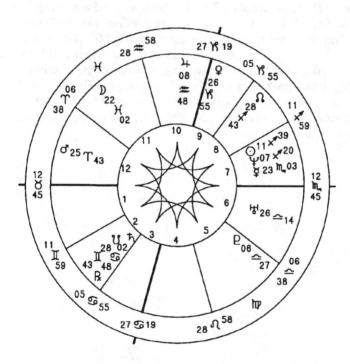

Example Chart #11:
3 Dec 1973 3:00 pm PST Los Angeles, CA 34N03 118W15
Move into house.

This couple lived in a beautiful house on a hill overlooking the ocean. He was a dentist and their family included three children ages five, six and eight. The littlest one had just started kindergarten and mother was going crazy driving them and picking them up, each one at a different time. They found a new house in the "flats" within walking distance of the elementary school. My client, the husband, was worried that this house, though pretty, would feel like a come-down.

To assuage his fears and make the new home as happy and carefree as possible, I calculated innumerable charts, until I decided on this one.

At 3:00 pm my client entered the house with a box of flatware; his wife proceeded into the kitchen and started lining drawers and cupboards. This action constituted "moving in."

The Moon is in the 11th house in Pisces and will trine Mercury, quincunx Uranus and last, but not least, sextile Venus. Venus rules the Ascendant (them) and the Moon rules their new home. The luminaries and benefics are elevated; Mars and Uranus are cadent and neither Saturn or Pluto is angular. This is about as good a moving-in chart as you will find. A Taurus Ascendant promises a solid and pleasant lifestyle. The chart ruler, Venus, is conjunct the MC, high enough in the chart for him to avoid a feeling of loss or status. Their children (5th) are represented by the Sun in fun-loving, optimistic Sagittarius.

They loved the house and the relaxed neighborhood; so did the children. The family stayed there for 13 years, until the youngest graduated and moved away to college. Now they live in a delightful home on the California coast.

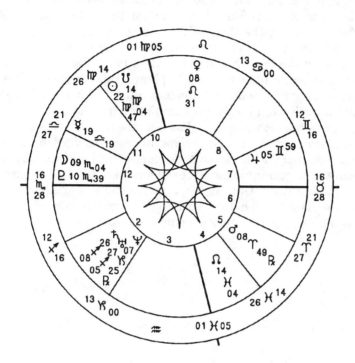

Example Chart #12:
15 Sep 1988 noon MSET Zurich, SWTZ 47N23 8E32
Move into apartment.

This Election chart is for the move of another young couple. The wife is my client. Her husband had just been transferred from London, England, to Zurich, Switzerland. They had found a lovely apartment and she was anxious to have a contented and lengthy stay. Timing was difficult since she was at the mercy of the movers as to which day the furniture would arrive and at the mercy of the landlord as to when he would turn over the key to her. Moving day was September 15th.

It was not easy to get the Moon past the quincunxes to Mars and Jupiter, as well as the square to Venus and conjunction to Pluto; to have a fixed Ascendant, the luminaries and benefics above the horizon and the difficult planets out of the angles.

Of the possible fixed Ascendants, Taurus rises before 6:00 am and Aquarius after 5:30 pm, before and after normal working hours. Scorpio was the only fixed sign that was possible and the approximate window was between 11:00 am and 1:00 pm. At 11:00 am 5 Scorpio was rising, the Moon was past the square to Venus by five minutes and

Pluto was in the 1st house. I felt that this move was intense enough with the Moon conjunct Pluto, but in the 1st house, it might be a bit too stressful. By 1:00 pm the Moon was still conjunct Pluto (Moon at 9 Scorpio 35, Pluto at 10 Scorpio 40) but now Mars was in the 4th house. By 3:15 pm, when the Moon had finally passed Pluto, Sagittarius was rising; Neptune and Pluto were angular; Mars, ruler of the 4th was past the sextile to Jupiter, now the Ascendant ruler. In other words, by eliminating one problem, I would have acquired a few others.

Except for the Moon/Pluto conjunction, the noon chart is a very good one. The Moon sextiles the Sun; Neptune, ruler of the 4th house sextiles Ascendant-ruler Pluto; the Ascendant-subruler Mars, has passed the square to Neptune; the benefics and luminaries are all elevated and neither Mars, Saturn, Uranus, Neptune nor Pluto is angular.

The couple are still living very happily in the apartment, though it looks as if he may get another transfer next year.

BUYING OR SELLING PROPERTY (HOUSE OR LAND)

TRADING PLACES

Much of what we have previously discussed also applies to **purchasing property.**

The Election chart to **purchase property** starts **the moment you make the official offer to buy,** whether to the seller directly or through a real estate agent. When you **sell property,** the Election chart starts **the moment you put the house up for sale,** either when you sign a contract with a realtor or when you hammer the sign into your front lawn; some people who sell without an agent feel the chart should be set for when they put a "For Sale" ad in the paper.

Rules For Election
To Buy Or Sell Property

1. Follow all the **usual rules for the Moon:** positive aspects, not void of course, and if possible, waxing. **Cancer** and **Taurus** Moons are particularly appropriate.

2. In any **purchase,** the **Ascendant** and its ruler describe the **buyer,** whereas the **Descendant** (7th) and its ruler denote the **seller.** Flowing aspects between these two houses are very beneficial for either a purchase or sale, but remember for whom you are calculating the chart, the seller or the buyer, and **fortify that house (1st) as well as the 4th house** which represents the property. **Smooth, positive aspects between these three houses (1st, 4th, 7th) are a must.**

In any **sale,** the **Ascendant** and its ruler describe the person who wishes to sell, the **Descendant** illustrates where the buyer is coming from. Easy aspects between these two houses help to make the deal flow smoothly.

3. **Look to the 4th to describe the house or land itself.** Try to **strengthen this astrological house and its ruler.** This applies to purchases as well as sales. I've seen sales fall through if the ruler of the 4th had only troublesome aspects or the Moon is void of course.

4. **To BUY, a fixed Ascendant is desirable,** unless this acquisition is to be for a quick turnover or a short term investment. **To SELL property quickly,** it is wise to choose a **cardinal Ascendant,** if possible; mutable is next best.

5. In any Election chart, it is helpful to **have the luminaries and benefics above the horizon** and the challenging planets (Mars, Saturn, Uranus and Pluto) away from the angles.

6. **Do not sign papers or contracts concerning any property if Mercury or Venus are retrograde.**

7. Avoid having the rulers of the angles in retrograde motion.

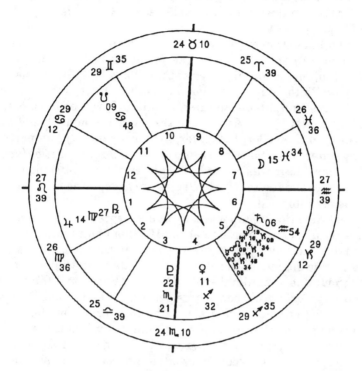

Example Chart #13:
9 Jan 1992 8:00 pm PST San Diego, CA 32N43 117W09
Offer to buy a house.

This client was very anxious to buy a house before his wife delivered their baby due in March. I told him to phone me any time he found a house he liked and I would quickly try to find a suitable time to make an offer, something I rarely do, since setting up a satisfactory Electional chart is usually a lengthy procedure. He called at 7:30 pm one January evening. I ran three charts, called him back and said, sign the offer now. Here is my reasoning:

The Moon at 15 Pisces had passed the opposition to Jupiter and was applying to a sextile to Neptune, its ruler, as well as a trine to Pluto, ruler of the 4th house illustrating the home. The Sun rules the Ascendant, representing my client and will sextile Pluto, ruler of the house he wants to buy. The Sun is past the conjunction to Neptune and Uranus, ruler of the 7th house, the seller, so there are neither positive nor negative aspects between seller and buyer. The Moon, always the prime factor in an Electional chart, is in the 7th house of the seller, and it describes what is happening...my client wants to buy something from the seller (7th) and what he wants (house/4th/Pluto), is in good aspect to the Moon.

The 1st house (buyer) is fortified because its ruler, the Sun, sextiles the 4th house ruler, Pluto, while the 7th house (seller) ruler, Uranus, will first conjunct Neptune, ruler of the seller's 2nd (8th of the chart), then sextile Pluto. Mars, subruler of the 4th, will conjunct Descendant ruler, Uranus, and 8th house ruler, Neptune. It will also trine Jupiter in the buyer's 1st house. As you can see, there are many beneficial aspects between the seller, the buyer, his money and the property. The applying square from Saturn to Pluto did not affect the parties for whom the Electional chart was erected. It could have brought some delays or annoyances to the realtor (Saturn rules the agent...the 6th house). If it did I was not informed.

In real time the Moon moves about one degree every two hours, so it will actually sextile Neptune about 10:00 pm and trine Pluto about 9:45 am the next day. When figuring timing in Electional charts, I usually figure one degree for the Moon equals a day, especially when dealing with mutable or cardinal signs. Mercury, Venus and the Sun actually move approximately one degree per day, so I often use the equivalent of one degree equals one week with those three planets. It is difficult to time the motion of the slower planets, unless there is a close aspect, within a degree or two, in which case it may take one or two months for an event to occur. Very often that is too long a time period for an Election chart to still be in effect.

In this chart you can see the significance of timing, because it shows that the 1st house (buyer) is stronger than the 7th house (seller) and that, in fact, some nebulous thing may happen to the seller in a little over two months when the Uranus/Neptune conjunction becomes exact. The seller had promised to make a few repairs in the kitchen; the plumber forgot to turn the water off; the kitchen flooded and the seller had to replace the entire kitchen floor. My client was, of course, delighted to get brand new linoleum.

There are some other strong points for the buyer in this chart: the benefics, Jupiter in the 1st and Venus in the 4th house, representative of the property. Since his wife was pregnant and because, in a way, they were buying the home because of the baby, it is most appropriate that the chart ruler, the Sun, is in the 5th house of children. The fixed Ascendant suggests they will live in the house for many years.

Although I was able to keep Mars, Saturn, Uranus, Neptune and Pluto out of the angles, I could not get the Sun, Venus and Jupiter above the horizon, but as I have reiterated, it is impossible to arrive at a perfect chart.

Another interesting factor to consider: my client was offering much less than the seller had asked. He questioned me as to when I thought the deal might be concluded. I examined the 2nd house, my client's money, ruled by Mercury, and the 8th house, the seller's money, ruled by Neptune. Mercury will conjunct Neptune within 16 degrees (equal to 16 days). Sure enough, after two weeks of haggling, the realtor called and said that the seller would sign the agreement. This type of reasoning does not always work; I was lucky.

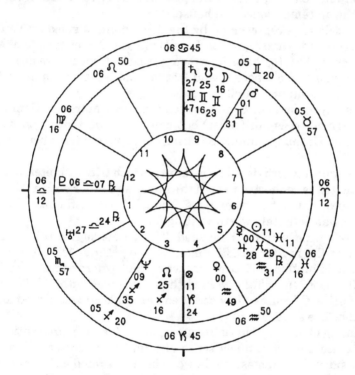

Example Chart #14:
1 Mar 1974 8:45 pm PDT Van Nuys, CA 34N11 118W27
Put house up for sale.

This couple unexpectedly found their dream house and made a quick offer to buy before the owner might change his mind. Now they were very worried if they could sell their house in time to make the down payment which was due within two months. Their worry was not without cause, since 1974 was still a buyer's rather than seller's market.

By now you are probably a pro at looking for Electional charts and realize that it takes a lot of searching to find the best possible time for a transaction, especially when you are searching for a good Moon and want the rulers of the Ascendant, Descendant and 4th house to interrelate favorably. Since they had only two months, and no house sells overnight, I really felt pushed. But I could not find any date that met the necessary parameters until March 1st, three weeks before their down payment on the new house was due, and while Mercury was still retrograde.

In the chart I finally decided upon, the Moon is at 16 Gemini and will trine Uranus, ruler of the 5th house (money from property); it will also conjunct Saturn, ruler of the property (4th house) and trine Jupiter in the aforementioned 5th house.

The seller, as represented by the Ascendant, is ruled by Venus in the 4th (property) at 0 Aquarius. It will trine the Descendant ruler Mars, the buyer, and Pluto, the seller's money, sextile Neptune (realtor), trine Uranus (money from house), and last but not least, for an extra bit of luck, Venus conjuncts Jupiter.

The buyer, depicted by the Descendant ruler Mars at 1 Gemini, not only is trined by Venus (seller) but will also trine Pluto, oppose Neptune, trine Uranus, conjunct Saturn (property) and trine benefic Jupiter.

The property (4th) is ruled by Saturn which trines Jupiter, but more importantly, is connected to both the buyer and seller with a trine from Venus and conjunction from Mars. Though it was difficult to find this chart, it was definitely worth waiting for.

Here's what actually happened. The couple signed the sales contract with the realtor at 8:45 pm on Friday, March 1st. Saturday the realtor held an "Open House" and when the owners came home in the late afternoon, two offers awaited them. One was within $1000 of the asking price. Of course, they accepted and the deal was signed and delivered before sundown.

Timing of any kind in Astrology is, at best, an iffy proposition. You need to use a lot of common sense and remember that cardinal signs are considered the fastest, so they can be interpreted as hours or days, Mutable signs are next fastest and could be considered days or weeks. The slowest signs are the fixed ones and usually can be translated as weeks and months. But as explained, basic common sense plays a large role here and depending on the event, instead of hours, days and weeks, you may be dealing with weeks, months and years. In other words, be careful and don't totally rely on timing to always work. Timing is not really a province of Electional charts; however, if a client for whom I have set up a "House for Sale" chart asks, "How soon do you think this property will sell?", I feel obligated to at least try to determine some framework of time.

In this case I was wrong. I figured 11 days, because the Moon was in a mutable sign and cadent house approaching a conjunction to Saturn, ruler of the property, in 11 degrees. Instead it just took one day, maybe because Venus ruling the seller, trined Mars, ruler of the buyer within less than a degree. I have learned to say very little about timing, unless my clients insist and then I do it reluctantly.

Though the natal charts of the couple were not really applicable, it made me feel good to see that the man's Ascendant happened to be the Ascendant of the Election chart. It provided confirmation that I was on the right track. Mercury retrograde played its usual tricks. The escrow company goofed and some of the papers had to be redone and resigned.

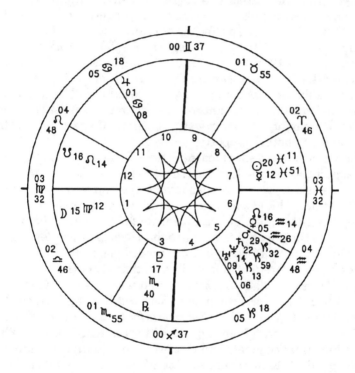

Example Chart #15:
10 Mar 1990 4:35 pm PST Malibu, CA 34N04 118W43
Put property up for sale.

A student wanted to sell a piece of property she owned. She had found a pretty good time; at least we both thought so.

As always, the Moon is my first consideration. It is in Virgo in the 1st house, past the opposition to Mercury. This is significant, since Mercury rules the Ascendant, my student, the seller of the property. The Moon sextiles Pluto, opposes the Sun, trines Saturn and its last aspect is a trine to Mars, ruler of the 8th house, the buyer's money (2nd from the 7th). The Ascendant ruler Mercury sextiles Neptune, ruler of the 7th (buyer in good aspect to seller). This aspect becomes exact in less than a degree and a half, and Mercury will eventually trine Pluto and sextile Saturn and Mars.

The 4th house (property) is ruled by Jupiter. The five personal planets are all past Jupiter which will in time oppose Uranus, Neptune, Saturn and trine Pluto. The important equation here is that the only connection from the property (Jupiter/4th) to the seller (Mercury/1st) and buyer (Neptune/7th) is a 13 degree opposition (Jupiter/Neptune).

The first serious prospect looked at the property on the morning of March 29th and he made an offer the next afternoon. The seller counter-offered on April 7th; the buyer accepted the offer on April 9th; escrow was opened April 12th. On May 11th, the buyer asked for a six month extension, based on a *Los Angeles Times* article on earthquakes which cited the Malibu area as being on a possible earthquake fault. On May 16th at 10:30 am the buyer canceled the escrow. The seller later discovered that the earthquake story was a screen for the fact that the buyer had purchased another property.

There is a lot of excellent learning here. I was in hopes that the nice lunar aspects, especially its final trine to Mars, along with the Mercury/Neptune sextile, would compensate for the Jupiter/Neptune opposition. It did not. The Moon is the primary consideration in Electional astrology, but though it may compensate for no aspects between the property and the buyer, it is not enough to overcome challenging ones.

In the beginning of this book, I reminded you to observe if a planet changes signs before the Moon will aspect it. This chart is a typical example. Mars is at 29 Capricorn 31 and it was necessary to make sure it was still in Capricorn when the Moon reaches that degree. In the ephemeris I use (*The American Ephemeris for the 20th Century*), it shows that the Moon switches from Virgo into Libra on March 11th at 3:39 pm GMT, while Mars changes from Capricorn to Aquarius on March 11th at 3:55 pm GMT, 16 minutes after the Moon reaches 0 Libra. In other words, the Moon/Mars trine is valid in this chart and had no negative bearing on the outcome.

BUYING A CAR

MERRILY WE ROLL ALONG

In California, as in other sprawled out communities, people live in their cars. Public transportation is minimal, distances are vast and automobiles are a necessity, not a luxury. Buying a car, even a used one, is not cheap and takes a good chunk out of anyone's salary. Many of my clients like to know a good time to buy a car, especially a new one.

When calculating the time for the purchase of a car, **the inception of the chart starts when you sign on the dotted line** and it makes no difference if you buy on the installment plan or pay cash.

1. As always, **the Moon** is the primary consideration, and all the **usual rules** are in effect. Additionally, if you wish to keep your car for a while, opt for a **fixed Moon.**

2. Just as with any other purchase, **the Ascendant** and its ruler describe the buyer, while the **Descendant** and its ruler denote the seller. In order to get a good deal if you are the buyer, you want your planets **to be stronger than those of the seller.**

3. If the **ruler of the 3rd house** (car) **and the 2nd** (money spent on it) **are in easy aspect** to the **Ascendant** (you) or each other, it generally indicates a good buy at a reasonable price.

4. If you are purchasing a luxury car avoid a **retrograde Venus** and do have **Venus in flowing aspect to the Ascendant** (buyer).

5. It is not wise to sign any contract when Mercury is retrograde, and buying a car on installment is a type of contract. But even if you pay cash, the car is a 3rd house entity and thus, in the flat chart, Mercury-ruled; so, if you can, **avoid a retrograde Mercury.**

6. It is also expedient to **avoid Mars retrograde** when buying anything mechanical or related to machinery, which, of course, includes automobiles.

7. Though it always helps to have the luminaries and benefics elevated, it is not the most important consideration here.

As always, practice makes perfect, so here are two car purchase charts.

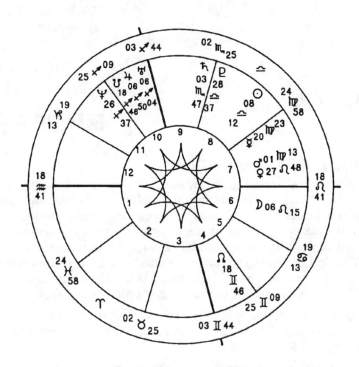

Example Chart #16:
1 Oct 1983 4:20 pm PDT Beverly Hills, CA 34N04 118W24
Buying new car.

The client was not in a big rush and gave me two weeks to find a good time slot to buy a new car. This was most helpful, as was the fact that car dealers and sales offices are open on weekends in California, which gave me extra days to work with. My client is a computer programmer; she services large companies all over California and spends a lot of time traveling long distances. She was looking for a heavy duty car. This is the chart I came up with.

The Moon in Leo (fixed sign) trines Jupiter and Neptune (ruler of the 2nd), sextiles the Sun, conjuncts Venus (ruler of the 3rd, the car) and its last aspect is a sextile to Pluto, ruler of the 9th house (long distance travel). A very fine Moon, indeed.

The car, represented by the 3rd house of the chart, is ruled by Venus which makes only one aspect, a sextile to Pluto describing the long distance travel of the 9th house. Uranus, ruler of the Ascendant (buyer) eventually conjuncts the 2nd house (money) ruler Neptune.

Since there is never a perfect chart, a few concessions had to be made. The fixed Ascendant in Aquarius ensures that the car will last for a while. Its ruler, Uranus, conjuncts Neptune ruler of the 2nd house of money, which suggests she would not have to pay an exorbitant price for the car (she didn't). Uranus also sextiles Pluto in the regenerative 8th house, indicating good service on her long hauls (Pluto rules the 9th). But Uranus (buyer) is squared by Mars which rules the 2nd house interception; it rules machinery in general and is placed in the 7th, representing the seller. The 7th house was stronger than I usually like, but you can't have everything.

The car is still driveable nine years later, though she now uses it as a second car when her newer one is in the shop and as a means of transportation for her daughter when she comes home from college. She was able to bargain for a good price, but in order to get a decent service contract, she had to commit to four years with the dealership which sold her the car. They turned out to have a miserable service and repair department and for four years she suffered through long delays, sloppy repairs and lots of aggravation (Mars square Uranus). The moment the contract expired, she went to her own mechanic who has kept the car in wonderful shape.

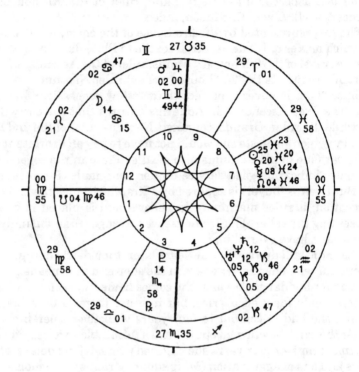

Example Chart #17:
15 Mar 1989 4:00 pm PST Los Angeles, CA 34N03 118W15
Purchase of a Rolls Royce.

This client presented me with an unusual problem. He had a chance to buy a classic Rolls Royce which needed some work. Being a classic car buff, he knew where to get the necessary parts and could do much of the repair himself. His problem was the money. Classic Rolls Royces cost a lot (this one was offered for $150,000 — supposedly a steal). My client wanted a time to buy which would, if possible, assure a future sale at a good profit. My time window was 10 days. Here's what I was lucky to find.

The Moon, as you well know by now, is always the most significant factor. Here it is in the 11th house in Cancer and will trine Pluto, Venus and the Sun. In this case I did not want a fixed Moon, since my client wanted a relatively quick resale. Either cardinal or mutable signs are more acceptable under those circumstances.

A fixed Ascendant was not desirable either, so I opted for Mutable Virgo with its ruler, Mercury, sextile Neptune ruling the 7th (future buyer) and trine Pluto, ruler of the 4th, the profit from the car (3rd).

Mercury will also conjunct Venus (ruler of the car — the 3rd) and the Sun. The car as stated is represented by Libra, ruled by Venus which is conjunct Mercury, ruling the Ascendant (buyer) and the 2nd (cost of the car.) Venus, which is exalted in Pisces, is trined by the Moon and will conjunct the Sun, a very strong Venus, indicating a worthy car and a fair price.

When money is to be made, received or earned from anything, look to the 2nd house. Here the money the buyer expects to make is from the car (3rd), so the 4th house (2nd from the 3rd) comes into play as the possible profit. Scorpio is on the cusp, the ruler Pluto is in the 3rd (car) and is trined by the Moon, sextiled by Uranus (ruler of the 6th, the work the client would do on the car), Neptune and Saturn, and trined by Mercury which rules him (Ascendant) and the cost of the car (2nd).

With these aspects, it seemed he could make money on the transaction. My only worry was that Mars, subruler of the 4th, at 2 Gemini, was not aspected by Venus (car) or Mercury (the buyer and the money involved). So the deal was dependent on the Mercury trine Pluto which would be exact in six degrees. Although mutable signs are considered fast, I knew the time frame was not six days or six weeks since the repairs would take longer than that. I was holding my breath that a resale would take place in six months and not in six years...

My client was able to finish the repairs in five months; he put the car on the market exactly six months after buying it and it took an additional six months to sell it. He made lots of money, since he sold it for $300,000 and his repairs, parts and labor only cost him $40,000.

STARTING A BUSINESS

MIND YOUR OWN BUSINESS

Except for dates and times to get married, most Electional astrologers are kept busy finding that special day or hour to start a business. Yet this is the hardest type of chart to pinpoint as far as rules are concerned, because different businesses are ruled by different planets... nothing simple like car/3rd house, home/4th house or partnership 1st/7th houses.

For example, a publishing house is ruled by Jupiter, and so is a bank, while a bookstore or doctor's office falls in Mercury's realm. A real estate office is Moon-ruled, as are restaurants and hotels; Venus rules gift stores and women's apparel, brokerages and brothels. Saturn has to do with the building trades, escrow, hardware stores, homeopathic shops and lumber yards; gambling joints and jewelry stores come under the Sun's auspices. So do motion picture theaters, while film *per se* and film laboratories are Neptune-ruled. Airplanes, airports, antique stores and garages are the domain of Uranus. Bakeries with their hot ovens fall under the aegis of Mars, while the yummy stuff they bake is Moon-ruled. Gun stores, gyms and tobacco stores are also Mars-ruled; Pluto is in charge of places that sell pornography, tombs, toilets or pest control. Of course, these are just some ideas to get you started. As stated on page 138, if in doubt, there are quite a few good books to help you with rulerships.

Any business starts when you unlock the door, let the first customer enter, cut a ribbon, toast with a glass of champagne, ring a bell or do whatever you choose which means you are now "in business."

A **corporation** (any business that is incorporated) **starts when the incorporation is approved by the state.** In many states the exact time is hard to pinpoint and noon charts have proven quite reliable. In some states the approval time is marked on the official stamp. In that case, of course, use the actual time as indicated.

Though the main electional rules are always the same, here are a few added directives to be taken into account in business set-up charts.

1. Though the **Moon**, because of its rapid movement through the chart, is still one of the most important considerations, in a business Electional chart it works nearly on a par with the **Sun**; you might even call **the luminaries co-significators.**

2. The **lunar rules** are the same; **avoid squares and a void of course Moon**; if possible, open or start the business on a **waxing Moon for growth.**

3. Although the **Ascendant** is meaningful and describes you if you own the project in question, the **Midheaven** is even more **crucial**, since it describes the business itself.

4. Nearly as noteworthy as the Midheaven which describes the business *per se*, is **the planet that rules the business in question.** It is best if that planet is **prominent and well aspected.**

5. For Electional business charts, **avoid** not only a **retrograde Venus**, but also a **retrograde planet ruling the business** and if there are papers to sign, of course, avoid **Mercury retrograde.**

6. Try to **place the Sun or the Midheaven ruler in the house that describes the goals of the business.** Want to make money? Go for an 11th house Sun. To enhance your reputation, put the Sun in the 10th house. Is your aim to distribute information? Opt for the Midheaven ruler in the 3rd. Again, your astrological knowledge and common sense will guide you.

7. As in all Electional charts it is **most beneficial if the Sun, Moon, Venus and Jupiter are elevated.**

8. In all business ventures **Saturn** is most influential and **should be well placed.** The **Sun** trine or sextile Saturn is particularly advantageous (effective organization and discipline.) Try to keep Saturn out of the angles, unless the business in question is Saturn-ruled or is owned and operated by a single individual.

9. The **Sun trine or sextile Jupiter is often invaluable for early success.** On the other hand, it is best to avoid troublesome applying aspects from the **Moon, Sun** and **Saturn** as well as the **Midheaven ruler,** to **Pluto** or **Neptune** within two degrees or the first two years. These transcendentals can pull a fledgling business down rapidly.

10. Use your astrological knowledge to deal with certain situations. Since **the Moon** plays such a substantial role in Electional astrology, its **po-**

sition by sign, house and aspect becomes doubly meaningful. A well-aspected **Moon** in **Taurus**, for example, could help assure monetary gains as well as steadfastness. In **Gemini** it may be ideal for publishing a magazine, but not as promising for a business that thrives on repetition and routine. The Moon in **Virgo** would be better for that. The Moon in **Leo** is super for ventures requiring extravagance, showmanship or advertising. A **Sagittarius** Moon is excellent for any business requiring salesmanship or travel, while in **Capricorn** it lends organizational skills. Endeavors needing initiative and daring are perfect for a Moon in **Aries**, whereas a store selling electrical appliances is ideal for an **Aquarian** Moon. A Moon in **Scorpio** is suitable for a mortuary business, while legal firms and beauty parlors do well with the Moon in **Libra**. Want to open a photographer's studio or a liquor store? Try a **Pisces** Moon. The Moon in **Cancer** is great for opening a restaurant, hotel or grocery store. The above are just a few suggestions to start you thinking.

To put all this into perspective, let's use a few illustrations. These charts are from the archives so you can judge the elements of success or failure through the passage of time.

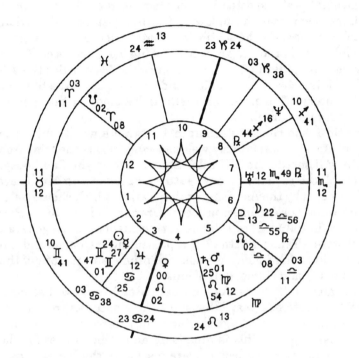

Example Chart #18:
16 Jun 1978 3:00 am EDT New York NY 40N45 73W57
Bookstore opening.

In May 1978, a writer who was a client called unexpectedly from New York. He was in the throes of buying an enormous library of antique and used books, many of them art books. He planned to take over the bookstore, and since quite a bit of money was involved, he was anxious to know if astrology could help.

The store was to close on Saturday, June 10th, 1978; my client and his partner needed to do a bit of renovation, add more books, change the decor and displays and open no later than Friday, June 16th. After calculating innumerable charts (all done by hand in those days), I found this reasonably good, but by no means perfect, chart.

Writers are an adventurous lot and my client did not even blink at my suggestion that they open the store at 3:00 am. "We'll invite a few friends, bring some bottles of champagne, break one on the door for good luck and drink the rest" was his comment.

Here are the "positive" and "not so positive" points of this chart. The Moon is in Libra; it is waxing and will trine the Sun as well as

Mercury and sextile Saturn. Mercury rules books; Saturn rules the Midheaven. A well-aspected Libran Moon in the 6th house describes smooth transactions with employees (6th) and pleasant interaction with the public in general. The sextile to the MC ruler, Saturn, augurs well for discipline and practical application of business practices. The Moon/ Sun trine is helpful in many areas...since the Moon rules the 4th, the actual building the shop occupies, and the Sun rules the 5th, the creative inventory. This aspect also reflects harmony in the operation of the business in general.

The **Sun** is in Gemini perchance, but what a wonderful placement for a bookstore. It is relatively well-aspected; beside the trine from the Moon, it will sextile the MC ruler Saturn and in the 2nd house, it is perfectly placed to make money. **Saturn, ruler of the MC**, is eventually conjuncted by the Ascendant ruler, Venus, which should help keep the purpose of the business in focus. Uranus and Neptune (Pisces is intercepted in the 11th) co-rule the **11th house** of income generated by the bookstore. Uranus is in the 7th, representing customers and is trined by Jupiter in the 3rd house of books. Neptune is in the 8th of the customer's money and is trined by Venus.

After almost 13 years, **Ascendant ruler Venus** will square Uranus, sextile Pluto one year later and trine Neptune three years after that. The Moon, the chart significator, trines Mercury, ruler of the business (books). Much of this is promising and compensates for the fact that the luminaries and benefics are not above the horizon, that neither the Sun nor the Moon are in the 3rd house of books, or for that matter in the 10th of the business; that there are no flowing aspects between the luminaries and Jupiter, and that I am not sure what the eventual (25 plus years) conjunction of Venus to Saturn will mean in 2003 or 2004.

The business is still in existence and has been very successful. In 1982, four years after they opened, when the Moon, which rules the 4th house, trined Mercury, they moved into larger facilities. In 1991, 13 years later, Venus, ruler of the Ascendant, squared the 7th house Uranus and my client's partner quit. In July 1992 he found a new partner. By then Venus sextiled Pluto, ruler of the partnership 7th house.

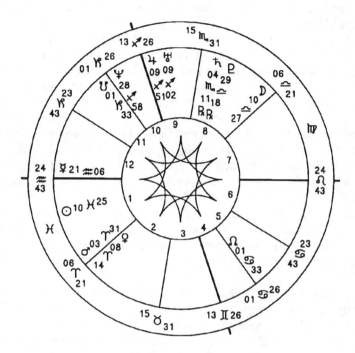

Example Chart #19:
1 Mar 1983 6:00 am PST Coeur d'Alene, ID 47N41 116W46
Restaurant Opening.

This chart points up the synchronicity of the universe, as well as what a successful Electional business chart looks like. Joan McEvers' family had decided to buy a breakfast and lunch restaurant called *Rustler's Roost*. Unfortunately, there was no choice as to which day or what time they could open after they took over. It had to be Tuesday, March 1, 1983 at 6:00 am, the usual time for the restaurant to open. As any good astrologer knows, at that time of the morning in March, the Sun will fall just behind the Ascendant, into the 12th house and no way did Joan even want to see a business chart with a 12th house Sun...so she never erected one.

Unaware of this story, I knew the *Roost* was a successful restaurant and figured it would be a good example to share with my Electional Astrology class. Was Joan surprised when I excitedly called to tell her that the Sun was in the 1st, not the 12th house.

The **Moon**, chart significator as well as ruler of food and restaurants, is in the 8th house and trines Mercury, ruler of the 4th/the restaurant building, as well as the intercepted 7th/the customers. In other words, harmonious relations are indicated in those areas, especially with the Moon in diplomatic Libra, so good at charming the clientele or employees, since it rules the 6th house. The trine to the Ascendant (owners) and sextile to the Midheaven (business) bode well for success. The Moon's sextile to Neptune in the 10th can be looked at in two ways...great for creating a charismatic atmosphere in the restaurant, attracting and charming customers, but also a warning signal to inspect all plumbing and water-connected machinery. Shortly after they opened, the big restaurant dishwasher broke down and had to be replaced at considerable cost. The Moon's last aspect, a conjunction to Pluto in the 8th house, denoted their ability to repay all loans, but can also suggest a deepening of support from others, as a well-aspected 8th house Moon would naturally indicate.

The all-important **Sun** is in the 1st house where the owners can put their personal stamp on their restaurant. It will make only one aspect, a wide square to Neptune (18½ degrees, equating to that many weeks months or years). The Sun has passed the squares to Uranus and Jupiter.

Jupiter ruling the Sagittarian **Midheaven** is in Sagittarius within four degrees of a conjunction to the MC. It will eventually sextile the Ascendant and Pluto and will conjunct Neptune in the 10th. With both the Ascendant and MC rulers conjunct in the 9th house, you can see that the Roost could attract a foreign clientele — in fact, many Canadians come to Coeur d'Alene and frequent the restaurant. You can also foresee from this aspect that the business (MC) should do well.

The Aquarius **Ascendant** (owners) is ruled by Uranus in Sagittarius conjunct MC ruler Jupiter. The owner and the business work as one, which is particularly helpful when more than one working owner (in this case, brothers) is involved. Uranus/Jupiter are well-aspected and will eventually conjunct Neptune and sextile Pluto.

Since the ability of the entrepreneur to make money is an important part of any successful business, the 2nd house should be carefully examined. Aries is on the cusp and the ruler Mars is in Aries in the 1st house (the owners will be personally instrumental in earning money). Mars trines MC and Ascendant rulers Jupiter and Uranus respectively, an ideal set-up for income potential. Much later Mars will trine Neptune and a year after that (could be 26 months or years) it will oppose Pluto. This opposition could herald a difficult period, possibly indicating too many expenditures, but with a basically positive Mars and Venus (always "benefic" in an Electional chart) in the 2nd house, any problems should be surmountable. Venus also trines the Jupiter/Uranus conjunction.

To let you know how this chart continues to work... when Jupiter moved to the MC, the younger brother, who had just moved back to town, went to work at the restaurant. This was quite fortunate, because when Uranus conjuncted the MC, the older brother got an offer he couldn't refuse and left for a three year period. In the spring of 1989, the owners were approached by a group of investors who wanted them to take over a larger building. Both brothers had had an eye on the location for several years and at last, were able to make a move which increased the business incredibly. The aspects were auspicious: Mars ruler of the 2nd trined the Ascendant and MC rulers and Venus had just passed the trine to the Midheaven. The Ascendant was trining the North Node in the 5th. This move has proved very successful and the family opened a second restaurant in July 1993.

If you would like even more insight into the details of this chart, look to the 3rd house for the environment/neighborhood, the 5th for creative endeavors which could range from decor to menu design and the food served, the 12th house for what goes on behind the scenes, probably in the kitchen and the deeper you care to dig, the more you can find out anything else you are curious about. Please realize that you do not need all this information to find a successful starting time, but it is available if you deem it necessary.

Example Incorporation Chart

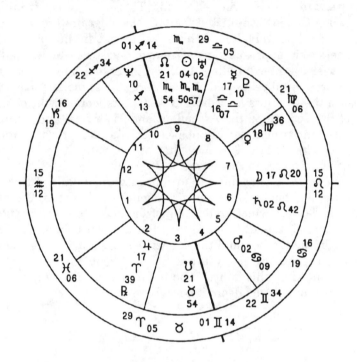

Example Chart #20:
28 Oct 1975 1:24 pm PST Encino, CA 34N10 118W30
Election for an incorporated organization.

This Electional Chart for the incorporation of Aquarius Workshops was chosen by a group; two rather experienced Electional astrologers, Robert C. Jansky and Betty Vander Beken, as well as Joan and myself, both good astrologers — but at that time not as experienced as the others. This organization was founded as an incorporated group, set up to have local monthly meetings geared to the astrological community, an astrological school and a quarterly magazine called *ASPECTS*. The key issue was astrological education.

There are two reasons I share this chart with you: a) Aquarius Workshops has endured for many years despite several ups and downs and b) the rules for an organization are slightly different from the usual electional rules and are therefore important for you to learn.

RULES FOR AN ELECTION CHART
FOR AN ORGANIZATION

These rules are spelled out by Rex Bills in *The Rulership Book* and are accepted with slight variations by most astrologers.

1st house — The membership, stockholders or personnel, whichever applies. Also the morale of the company or organization.

2nd house — Liquid assets, voluntary expenses, ability to earn money as well as the attitude toward earning money, and investments.

3rd house — Contacts with the public, internal communications.

4th house — Any real estate investments made by the organization; the base of operation; location and condition of office or building, if one is owned or used.

5th house — Executive personnel (except president and elected officials); the governing body; attitude or action by stockholders or board in opposition to president.

6th house — Workers, employees; possible labor problems or strikes.

7th house — Relations with other organizations, competitors and their activity; lawsuits and legal affairs.

8th house — Losses or gains (bequests) through death (and resignation). Company treasurer; revenue from investments or frozen assets.

9th house — The advertising department, long distance communications; results of mail order campaigns, publications, professional consultants; publicity and public relations.

10th house — The corporation, governing authority, president or chairman of the board.

11th house — Other friendly organizations; the part of the corporation which provides social activities; the treasury (money made by the corporation).

12th house — Enemies and secret organizations opposed to the corporation.

This chart is calculated for the signing of the incorporation papers by Joan McEvers, Sharon Culbreth and myself.

As you can see from the rules cited, when calculating an organizational chart, the corporation, in this case Aquarius Workshops, Inc., is depicted by the **10th house** not the 1st. You also find the President (or chairman of the board, whichever may apply) in this house. In this chart open and outgoing Sagittarius is on the MC; Jupiter which rules it is in the 2nd house of earning ability and is trined by the Moon and opposed by Mercury. Neptune, the planet of illusion and glamour, is in the 10th house.

Basically, Aquarius Workshops, as well as its president, should come across as glamorous, charismatic, and it should never have money problems. The Mercury/Jupiter opposition could indicate occasional withdrawal of support from others (8th) or misunderstandings with the board (5th) since Mercury rules the 4th, 5th and 8th houses.

The **11th house** not only represents other friendly organizations, but in an organizational chart, as the 2nd of the 10th it denotes "the treasury" or monies earned and received by the incorporated body. Sagittarius on this cusp, with Jupiter in the 2nd house, is a confirmation of excellent financial prospects. In this house the opposition (Mercury/Jupiter) could imply overly ambitious plans when dealing with other organizations and groups, or possibly a bit of a standoffish attitude toward them.

The **12th house** represents those opposed to the organization, or those who would mount behind-the-scenes actions. The ruler Saturn is in Leo in the 6th house of work and workers; it squares Ascendant-ruler Uranus and applies to a wide trine to Neptune in the 10th. The square to Uranus could signal that those who work for Aquarius Workshops might also undermine it. On the other hand, the trine to Neptune reflects great idealism and the ability to eventually make dreams a reality.

The **Aquarius Ascendant** well befits an astrological organization as does Uranus rising just ahead of the Sun in the 9th house of publications (*ASPECTS* Magazine) and adult education (Aquarius Workshops teaches grown-ups). Mars, ruler of the 3rd house of communication, trines Uranus — this organization has appeal to the public, its subscribers, members and students, especially those who enjoy the unconventional.

Jupiter in the **2nd house**, as already noted, is a bonus; the ruler, Neptune in the 10th may signify that the values of the leaders of the group are visionary and idealistic.

The **3rd house** is ruled by Mars in Cancer in the 5th with only one aspect, a trine to Uranus; Taurus is intercepted in the 3rd and Venus, its ruler, is in Virgo in the 7th house. Venus makes no applying aspects. With the rulers of the 3rd in the 5th (the board), trine the ruler of the Ascendant (the membership), and Venus in the 7th (other organizations), the founders felt that Aquarius Workshops should be able to get its message across easily and clearly.

Mercury in Libra in the 8th rules the **4th house**, the base of this corporation. Gemini on the cusp enjoys disseminating information which should serve the group well. In Libra, Mercury can inform others with tact and diplomacy; in the 8th house, it indicates support from others, especially those outside the organization. The opposition from Mercury to Jupiter, can however, denote overblown expectations of what the president (Jupiter rules the 10th) can or should do.

Mercury also rules the **5th house** which represents the Aquarius Workshops Board. It reflects the attitude as well as any action taken by the board against the president. This is the most difficult house in the entire chart; not only because the ruler opposes Jupiter, but because Mars is here. In any Electional chart Mars is considered a malefic planet; even in natal astrology we know that Mars suggests strife and misunderstandings. Here, however, Mars trines Uranus, the Ascendant-ruler, so the possible difficulties are tempered and the energies can be used positively to work for and with the membership at large.

Aquarius Workshops does not have paid workers; only volunteers as represented by the **6th house**. With Cancer on the cusp and the Moon ruling it trine Jupiter, much help should be available. But Saturn in this house suggests that a few very hardworking, devoted individuals are always there to help. It can also reflect Saturn's negative side, and the square to Uranus could indicate delays in finding volunteers.

Leo on the cusp of the **7th house** of competitors and relations with other organizations forecasts a strong Aquarius Workshops which may at times overwhelm other groups who could see it as showy, dramatic and interesting to the public at large, especially with the Moon in Leo in the 7th and the Sun which rules it in the 9th in close proximity to unconventional Uranus. Venus here may tone down some of the "here I am world" bearing, which is helpful in living up to their reputation.

The **8th house** connotes the organization's treasurer who must have a difficult time keeping finances in line, since ruler Mercury opposes Jupiter. The president and organization (10th) *per se* may see all the money held in assets and want to spend it; the treasurer says "whoa" since with Virgo-on-the-cusp exactitude s/he will do what is totally correct. Pluto in the 8th house intensifies these attitudes.

Last but hardly least, the **9th house** personifies the *raison d'être* for the organization, the quarterly magazine *ASPECTS*, the teaching outline and testing program conceived in order to eventually launch informed and well-versed astrologers. The Sun is in this house, lending it much strength; so is Uranus verifying that the teaching, publications and advertising generated through this house will not be run-of-the-mill and will fit a subject like astrology very well.

Aquarius Workshops has done well from its inception. Its presidents, including Joan and myself, were usually quite well known in astrological circles and respected for their expertise. *ASPECTS* magazine succeeded from day one and its subscriptions have kept the organization in the black. Their teachers use *The Only Way...* series for beginning and intermediate students and they have an excellent reputation as a School of Astrology. Actually everything functions pretty much as the Electional chart indicates, including the fact that the board often does not see eye-to-eye with the presiding officer.

Please keep in mind that the above example chart was for the election of the original corporation. Once such a corporation exists and you become a member of it, you view the chart through the lens of the Ascendant, whether you are a board member (originally 5th house) or the president (originally 10th house).

ELECTION FOR SURGERY

THIS IS YOUR LIFE

An electional chart for surgery presents a serious problem... in most cases surgery is not optional, and must nearly always be performed at the convenience of the doctor, hospital or surgical team. Even if you have a choice, such as when the doctor says: "Sometime next week" or "Within the next few days," don't get too excited; the carefully chosen 2:35 pm may not fit the doctor's schedule. He may have an emergency or the operating room may not be available. The promised 8:00 am more often than not turns out to be 8:30 or 9:00 am. Under these circumstances, it may not be worthwhile to erect a timed Electional chart.

But there are some plans you can make if you have the choice of, at least, the **day.** There are many circumstances you can **avoid.** Most of them are based on some of the general rules cited at the beginning of the Electional segment of this book; the rest are based on astrological knowledge.

1. Try to **avoid surgery when the transiting Moon is in the sign relating to the area of the body** being operated on:

Remember: the Moon spends no more than two and a half days in each sign, making it not too difficult, in most cases, to postpone surgery.

ARIES rules the head area including the face, brain and upper teeth. With the Moon here, it is not a good time to correct a deviated septum or have a cataract removed.

TAURUS rules the throat, neck, ears, vocal chords, thyroid, tonsils and lower teeth. A tonsillectomy or a mastoidectomy are ill-advised when the Moon is here.

GEMINI rules the lungs, collarbone, hands, arms, shoulders and nervous system. A student broke his arm skiing; aware of Electional rules, he opted to wait five hours for the Moon to reach Cancer before he had his arm set. The operation was successful.

CANCER rules the breast area, stomach, upper lobes of the liver, the esophagus, pancreas and internal reproductive organs as well as the disease cancer. If possible, avoid a mastectomy or an abortion when the Moon is in this sign.

LEO rules the heart and its diseases, aneurysms, the back, including the spine and dorsal region and the sides of the body. You are allowed to lose your heart with the Moon in Leo, but don't have open-heart surgery.

VIRGO rules the intestines, lower lobes of the liver, the bowels, appendix and solar plexus. Try to postpone diverticulitis surgery until the Moon has left Virgo.

LIBRA rules the kidneys, lower back, buttocks, lumbar region, ovaries and the veins in general. It is all right to go to a chiropractor to have your back adjusted while the Moon is in Libra; adjustments are not surgery.

SCORPIO rules the genitals, bladder, rectum, external reproductive organs, adenoids, the colon, groin and hemorrhoids. If possible postpone a D & C, rectal surgery or bladder repair until the Moon has reached some other sign.

SAGITTARIUS rules the hips, thighs, upper leg, arteries and blood in general as well as the sacral region of the body. If you can, avoid hip replacement surgery with the Moon in this sign.

CAPRICORN rules the knees, lower leg, skin, bones and cuticles. It also rules the teeth. Even removal of cartilage in the kneecap, which nowadays can be done by laser, is better postponed for a few hours until the Moon has left this sign.

AQUARIUS rules the ankles, shins, blood circulation and varicose veins. When the Moon is here, it is not a good time for a hamstring or an Achilles tendon operation.

PISCES rules the feet and toes. Don't worry about having a pedicure, but do sidestep a bunion removal until the Moon moves out of Pisces.

2. The **transiting Moon in Scorpio** has proven to be **unfavorable** for any sort of surgery.

3. It is **better to not to have the Moon applying to square any planet,** especially the malefics. Lunar oppositions do not seem to create major problems.

4. If possible, **avoid surgery on a Full Moon.** Statistics show that more bleeding occurs during this time. The **New Moon** phase is good for many types of surgery, but those involving veins, arteries or the heart are best performed on a **waning Moon.**

5. There is **controversy** among astrologers about having surgery on a **void of course Moon.** A Cancer biopsy where you hope "nothing will come of it" may be appropriate on a void Moon. However, removing a cancerous growth, in my opinion, should not be performed when the Moon is void of course.

6. A **retrograde Mercury is ill-advised** for any type of surgery, since some part or even all of it may have to be redone.

7. It is **not a good idea to have cosmetic surgery when Venus is retrograde.**

8. Mars rules the surgery as well as the surgeon, therefore try to **avoid Mars retrograde** or the outcome of the operation may not be as you expect, and often is unfavorable. (The surgeon is also depicted by the 7th house.)

9. What you *do* want are **harmonious aspects to the Sun** (strength-giving) and **Moon, to the planet ruling the surgery in question, to the ruler of the 8th house** (surgery), **or the Ascendant** (physical body). A strong **Jupiter** can be very protective.

10. **Do not worry if transiting Mars is passing through your natal 8th house, or is heavily involved by progression, direction or transit to the Sun, Ascendant or 8th house ruler.** That just shows that surgery may be indicated.

OTHER ELECTIONAL OPTIONS

As you actively engage in Electional Astrology, you will encounter questions in areas that you have never thought of before and none of your reference books will have the directions and answers you are looking for. That is when you will really learn, because you have to dig down into your own knowledge and with common sense and logic try to find the right response.

You can, of course, just explain your lack of practice in the area questioned, but most of my clients insist I try anyway, and frankly, there is great learning in anything new you try. So here are some thoughts on possible Electional questions with answers based more on logic than actual experience.

Trips: On The Road Again

Many people ask for an Electional chart when they go on a trip. When I first started doing this kind of astrology, I eagerly obliged and anxiously awaited feedback, something I zealously seek, since it is the best way to learn. It did not take me very long to find out that **trip charts** are not very effective. First of all, you have absolutely no control over when your plane, train or bus will depart, so you have to figure the chart for the time you leave your house. Secondly, I notice that many aspects involving the so-called malefics did not turn out as expected.

A client's son made a solo trip to Europe, a high school graduation gift from his parents. The chart for his departure showed Mars square Pluto. Mars ruled the 3rd house of transportation; Venus, ruler of the 9th of long trips, was within a one degree square to Uranus. Aquarius was rising and the chart ruler Uranus was in the 9th house. Try as I might, I could not change the chart to my liking, unless I suggested the boy should leave the house the night before, and even then Mars was still square Pluto, but the houses involved would not be trip-related.

I truthfully told my client the quandary I was in. She decided that leaving the house the night before was much too complicated; her son left in the morning and we both held our breath! He arrived in Paris where he was supposed to change planes and continue to Italy to the home of a relative. But, as frequently happens in France and Italy, there was a local strike and there were neither planes flying nor trains running for 48 hours. The "poor" boy had to spend two days in Paris, a real "punishment" for an 18-year-old. Mars, ruling the 3rd house, square Pluto indicated nothing more than an interruption in the transportation system.

A few other misleading incidents as well as many talks with Joan, who had similar experiences, led both of us to decline erecting "trip" charts. There are also a few philosophical reasons not to calculate them. Astrology is supposed to help you better your life by understanding your natal chart; to grasp the right moment for change, action or learning by studying and comprehending your chart moved forward to a specific year; to find the proper point in time to undertake an important venture by erecting an Electional chart...but a trip really fits none of these propositions; it is not usually an all-important or life-changing project.

Just as significant, in my opinion, is the fact that when you have to turn yourself into a pretzel, like leaving the house at some ridiculous hour, staying who-knows-where, your clothes packed into a suitcase even longer than necessary, all in order to depart on a different astrological chart, then astrology has ceased to be your helper; you have become its slave.

Lawsuits: To Sue Or Not To Sue

1. The **Ascendant**, its ruler and planets in the 1st house **denote the person who initiates the lawsuit.**

2. The **Descendant**, its ruler and planets in the 7th house **depict the opponent.**

3. **If you wish the initiator to win, fortify the Ascendant.** A strongly placed **Mars** and **Pluto**, representing assertion and sometimes aggressiveness, are helpful; so are **Aries** or **Scorpio** rising, especially when well-aspected.

4. **Try to have the Ascendant ruler stronger than the Descendant ruler.** That can be by dignity, high focus, aspects etc. The reverse applies, of course, if you wish the other party to win.

5. As always in Electional Astrology, the **Moon is most crucial,** so follow all the previously established lunar rules.

6. **Keep Saturn out of your client's 12th house**; it is the house of secrets and hidden enemies and Saturn there can bring out unwanted testimony in the courtroom.

In my entire astrological career, I've only twice been asked a time to sue someone. In one case it was settled out of court. In the other case, my client won. But that is not enough of a sampling for me to feel even halfway sure that my approach is the right one. Joan and I pride ourselves that every word we have written in our seven books is based on actual empirical experience, not repetition of aphorisms handed down through the ages. When we state that the Moon square Uranus often manifests as high-strung, it is because we have observed this in hundreds of cases, not because we read it in some astrological book. We hope you will do the same.

Applying For A Job:
Work Makes The World Go Around

Here's another area I shy away from, because people so often are in for a disappointment. It is rare that your future boss lets you pick the time for an interview; it is even rarer that s/he will see you exactly at the appointed time. But should all the ideal circumstances occur, here is what you might aim for.

1. As always, find a day where the **Moon has no squares** until it changes sign.

2. When looking for a job, you are represented by the **Ascendant.** Try for a **well-aspected Ascendant,** Ascendant ruler or, if possible, place **Jupiter or Venus in the 1st house.**

3. **Positive aspects between the Ascendant/you and the 6th house/** the job are most helpful.

4. The boss or superior is denoted by the **10th house.** Try to arrange some **harmonious connection between the Midheaven or its ruler and the Ascendant.**

5. Some job applicants want to come across in a specific way, in which case it might be wise to opt for **an Ascendant in the sign of the zodiac that gives you that certain appearance you want**; just realize the sign you are opting for may rise at midnight! In other words, you can't always have everything the way you would like it. Here are some keywords that fit the Ascendant sign: Assertive/Aries, free and breezy/Sagittarius, organized/Capricorn, able to grasp new concepts/ Aquarius, charming/Libra, intellectually alert/Gemini, dramatic/Leo, sensitive and imaginative/Pisces, steadfast/Taurus, neat and careful/ Virgo, dedicated/Cancer, assured and incisive/Scorpio.

CONCEPTION AND FERTILITY ELECTIONS

ROCK-A-BYE BABY

This is an area that many astrologers have dabbled with, but to the best of my knowledge very little has been written about it. A fascinating realm of astrology, yet this is one that needs to be approached with GREAT caution. Though I have worked with conception charts and related fields for more than 20 years, I learn something new with every horoscope, and as the medical field pioneers new methods day after day, to the point where a woman even after menopause can give birth, we in the astrological world have to keep in step. Thus, regard this chapter only as an overture, with the opera still to be written.

First of all we need to divide that which we do know into three parts:

1. **Birth control** as based on the *Fertility Cycle*.

2. **The best time to become pregnant** based on the astrological fertility cycle, as well as on the woman's natural ovulation cycle.

3. **Pregnancy charts** based on the latest medical advances in child conception.

The Fertility Cycle

The ancients established that there seemed to be a connection between the distance from the Sun to the Moon in a woman's chart and fertility. Just as the female body experiences the menstrual cycle, so the natal chart seems to indicate those times when a woman is most receptive to pregnancy, namely that moment approximately once a month when the Sun is at the same distance from the Moon as it is at birth. For example, if your natal Sun is at 15 Cancer 40 and your natal Moon is at 23 Scorpio 55, the distance between the luminaries is 128 degrees and 15 minutes. Approximately every 30 days the Sun and Moon will be at a point where they are separated by 128 degrees and 15 minutes.

Dr. Eugen Jonas, a gynecologist and astrologer from the former republic of Czechoslovakia, worked with this fertility cycle in his astrological birth control clinic for many years and supposedly helped women to conceive as well as prevent conception. This latter theory was particularly intriguing to modern couples who wanted to freely pursue sexual activity without resorting to such intrusive measures as birth control pills or intrauterine devices.

Birth Control

Some astrologers have assumed that if you know the day of your greatest fertility, by adding two or three days before and after, you have secured a fertile period and therefore the remaining days of the cycle should be infertile and safe. Please understand right up front that **this method of birth control is totally unreliable and is not recommended.**

In today's world where the average woman has taken many artificial substances, from aspirin to birth control pills, there are very few whose natural cycle coincides with her astrological one and the expected "safe" times may be when her natural ovulation takes place, a great time to get pregnant!

Even if you are fortunate enough to be in synchronicity with nature, nobody can predict exactly how long it takes the semen to travel up the birth canal to inseminate the egg or, at times, "lay in wait" in the tubal area for the egg to be receptive. Medicine says the semen can live for 48 hours, but some doctors report that they know of cases where insemination took as much as 60 hours, thus the *safe day* count can be off. Of course the same thing can happen when your usually regular ovulation occurs a day early or late, but that is a natural problem, not an astrological one. In other words, do not use this fertility cycle to ensure birth control.

The Best Time to Become Pregnant

So why do I burden you with all this useless knowledge? Because the other side of the coin, namely the time to get pregnant, has proven to be most helpful. I have worked with the "fertility cycle" for many years and have had some very positive results. Please understand, this has **nothing** to do with the **birth** of the child, only the **pregnancy** of the mother.

About 20 years ago when I first became interested in this fertility cycle, I had many young women clients who wanted to get pregnant at certain times which fit into their work schedule, such as teachers who wished for a summer baby, and my role was simply to find their fertile days for October or November. There were quite a few clients who did not want too much time to lapse between their first and second child; those who had lost a baby during pregnancy and wanted my help to avoid a repetition; and some women who had trouble conceiving.

Though I have had many successes, I have also had failures and more than anything else, I have learned great respect for nature and am sure that if something does not succeed, it is often because it is not supposed to. Therefore, I never promise results, I only offer to try and help to the best of my ability. The nicest part of this astrological method is that the client does not have to undergo any medical procedure; there are no pills to be taken, no diets to adhere to...the only demand is to have sex at a certain time, and that is not usually considered a hardship. As a result I have been able to make quite a few astrological and psychological deductions which have helped many clients achieve a viable pregnancy.

The mechanics of calculating fertility cycles are very easy; ACS will send you dates and times for one year; some astrological software programs can do it, or you can figure it manually like we did BC (before computers). On page 195 you can see what my fertility data sheet looks like. It prints out 13 dates for one year and the time on each day when the fertility cycle peaks, which is the exact moment when the Sun and Moon are equidistant to their position at birth.

Once you have this data, it is necessary to run charts for all 13 dates. Be sure to calculate which time zone your client will be in for the year and if the couple travel, adjust the times given accordingly.

Natural ovulation, the time when the egg is ready to be impregnated, lasts about one day; most doctors figure around 20 hours. To be on the safe side, I tighten the astrological period to 12-14 hours or 6-7 hours on each side of the optimum moment. After carefully studying the charts, I consult with the client as to which of the 13 possible days are most likely to be productive, which are only fair and those which I consider problematic...those when the Moon squares Mars or Uranus or opposes Saturn.

The **Rules** for interpreting a fertility chart are very simple. It is, in its own way, a type of Electional chart, and since we are dealing with conception, **everything** is based on the Moon. Primarily, you must check all the applying aspects the Moon makes in the chart and secondarily, the aspects it makes to the natal chart. Since learning is easiest with examples, let's look at a fertility cycle I prepared for a client in 1976.

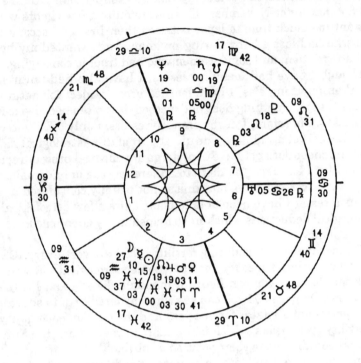

Example Chart #21:
6 Mar 1951 2:48 am PST Los Angeles, CA 34N04 188W15
Mindy/Natal

My client, Mindy, had been married for two years. She had worn an intrauterine coil which had led to bleeding and once it was removed, she could not seem to become pregnant. She had moved from California to Switzerland, which had added physical and emotional stress, often a reason for not being able to conceive. As I do with every client, I counseled that she follow her natural ovulation cycle with a temperature chart or however her doctor suggested and take advantage of that day as well.

Here is the actual list as it prints out the data:

Mindy: Fertility Dates for MET (-1 Zone) August 1976 - August 1977

> 08-24-1976 at 03h27m20s (Chart #22)
>
> 09-22-1976 at 13h45m33s (Chart #23)
>
> 10-21-1976 at 23h45m58s (Chart #24)
>
> 11-20-1976 at 09h52m11s
>
> 12-19-1976 at 20h11m06s
>
> 01-18-1977 at 06h50m41s
>
> 02-16-1977 at 18h14m21s
>
> 03-18-1977 at 06h53m23s
>
> 04-16-1977 at 21h02m14s
>
> 05-16-1977 at 12h20m27s
>
> 06-15-1977 at 04h01m43s
>
> 07-14-1977 at 19h21m09s
>
> 08-13-1977 at 09h55m37s

The first chart on this list is for August 24, 1976, at 3:27 am MET (-1 zone) for Zurich, Switzerland . Since Switzerland observes daylight saving time in August, I used 4:27 am MEDT. (See Chart #22). Though computers and software programs are quite reliable, we who input the data are human and as such we do occasionally err. **Make sure that the distance between the Sun and Moon is the same as it is in the natal chart.** Mindy's natal separation is 17 degrees and 54 minutes. It should be the same in every fertility chart you calculate for her. The distance from the Moon at 13 Leo 09 to the Sun at 1 Virgo 03 is 17 degrees and 54 minutes. (A one minute difference often exists because most computer programs do not print out seconds for the Sun or Moon, automatically rounding up or down.) In chart #23 the Moon is at 11 Virgo 44, the Sun at 29 Virgo, 38, a distance of 17 degrees 54 minutes.

Although the Moon is only at 13 Leo, it makes only one applying aspect, a trine to the MC. It is 3 degrees and 21 minutes (approximately seven hours) past a conjunction to Saturn. I suggested that they should not have intercourse before 10:00 pm the evening before, after the Moon passed Saturn, and everything was fine through 10:00 am on the 24th. That provided a 24 hour window. The Moon at 13 Leo falls into Mindy's natal 8th house; it will quincunx the natal Sun, conjunct Pluto, sextile Neptune, quincunx Jupiter, oppose the Moon and its last aspect is a sextile to the MC. I consider this an okay chart, not particularly good or bad. I prefer more action in the fertility chart and I am not keen on the opposition to the natal Moon, but none of it is so problematic that I

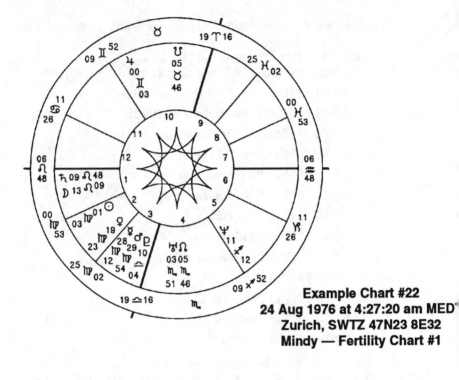

Example Chart #22
24 Aug 1976 at 4:27:20 am MED'
Zurich, SWTZ 47N23 8E32
Mindy — Fertility Chart #1

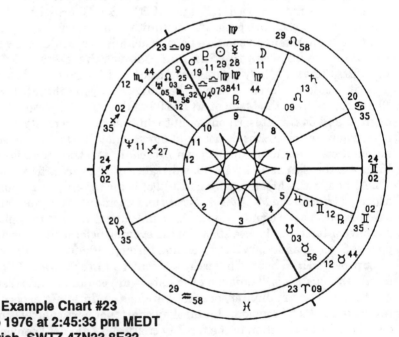

Example Chart #23
22 Sep 1976 at 2:45:33 pm MEDT
Zurich, SWTZ 47N23 8E32
Mindy — Fertility Chart #2

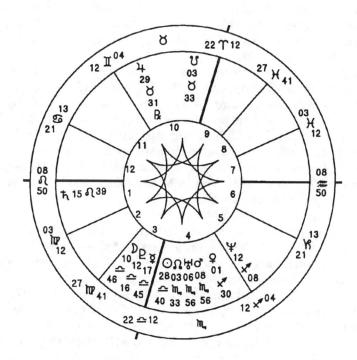

Example Chart #24
21 Oct 1976 at 11:45:58 pm MET
Zurich, SWTZ 47N23 8E32
Mindy — Fertility Chart #3

would counsel Mindy to skip that particular date. Result — she did not get pregnant.

The second date on the chart (#23) is for September 22, 1976, at 2:45:33 pm MEDT for Zurich. Here the Moon is at 11 Virgo, just past the square to Neptune by 17 minutes or less than one hour in clock time. The Moon applied to a square to the Ascendant, a conjunction to Mercury and last but not least, a conjunction to the Sun. Natally the Moon still falls in Mindy's 8th house and will quincunx Venus and oppose the Sun as well as Jupiter. Again, not a great chart. I was particularly worried about the square to the Ascendant (her body) but we could not wait for the aspect to pass, since moving the Moon 11 plus degrees takes 22 hours, longer than the fertile period is in effect. I needn't have worried... Mindy's husband was called out of town on business so nothing happened! Nothing happened during her ovulation period either.

The third date (Chart #24) October 21, 1976, at 11:45:58 pm MET shows the Moon at 10 Libra. Have you noticed how the Moon is always in the following sign and a bit earlier than the month before? (13 Leo in August, 11 Virgo in September and 10 Libra in October.) This is the normal pattern for fertility charts.

In this chart, the Moon sextiles Neptune, conjuncts Pluto, sextiles Saturn, conjuncts Mercury, opposes the MC and finally there is a lovely conjunction to the Sun, ending with a quincunx to Jupiter. I really liked this chart and though I am not always fond of Pluto's intensity in Electional charts, I feel Moon/Pluto conjunctions are positive for fertility purposes. After all, Pluto rules the generative area (8th house) in the flat chart. I wondered about the opposition to the MC in 11½ degrees.

The fertility chart Moon was in Mindy's natal 9th house, ready to oppose Venus, quincunx the Sun, sextile Pluto, quincunx Jupiter and ends with a trine to natal Moon. Quite nice.

Mindy got pregnant on October 21st. She fell from a step-stool while painting the future baby's room on January 8, 1987 — exactly 11½ weeks after conception (Moon opposed MC, the aspect I was concerned about). Thank God she was not seriously hurt, a painful ankle, but the baby was not affected. She had a strapping baby boy on July 10, 1977.

Two questions I hear again and again: "Can we predict the baby's gender?" and "Can we predict anything about the baby from the conception chart?" After carefully comparing about 75 birth and conception charts, not an in-depth study of thousands, but enough for a start, I must say that I see **nothing** that links one chart with the other. Not the conception Moon to the natal Moon, the Ascendant to the luminaries or any other links to the conception chart and that of the child. As to pre-determining the baby's gender — the answer is "yes" and "no." If you refer to the conception chart #24 for October 21st, you will note that the Moon was in Libra, a "male" sign astrologically speaking. If insemination takes place while the Moon is in Libra, Aries, Gemini, Leo, Sagittarius or Aquarius, the baby should be male. Unfortunately we **do not know** when insemination takes place. As I previously said, it can take the semen more than 48 hours to fertilize the egg; in that time span the Moon may have entered the next, feminine sign. The answer at best is "maybe."

Second Fertility Study

Another interesting fertility case was that of a charming Greek woman, Marissa, who was living in Monte Carlo in the summer of 1980 when she consulted me.

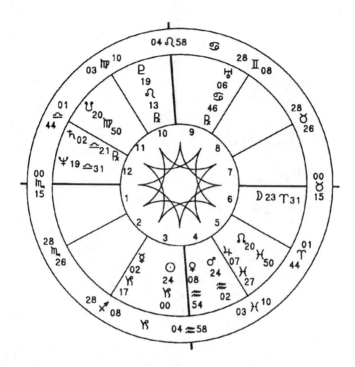

Example Chart #25:
15 Jan 1951 at 1:20 am EET (-2) in Athens, Greece 37N58 23E43
Marissa/Natal

Monaco may be an exquisite place, but it has a pretty bad reputation when it comes to medical care. Marissa had a four-year-old son and had been trying to conceive again since early 1978 with no success. Both she and her husband had been tested and found okay. When I calculated her fertility cycle, we discovered that most of the peak days seemed to fall during those weeks when she was expecting her period, which had been pretty regular.

Of the 13 dates, only two were really favorable. This unfortunately can happen and, in fact, once I had to tell a client that the year she had chosen had only one "good" date.

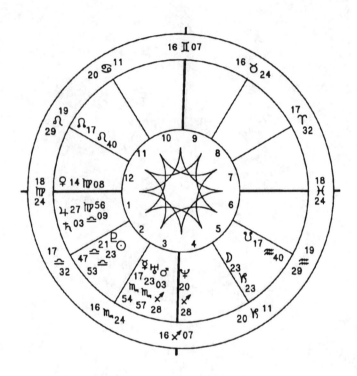

Example Chart #26:
17 Oct 1980 at 3:47 am MET in Monte Carlo, Monaco 43N45 7E25
The first "favorable" time for Marissa.

The Moon at 23 Capricorn 23 will, of course, square the Sun, as it should, since that is the distance between the natal luminaries. After that it sextiles Uranus and trines Jupiter, nice aspects for a conception chart. Natally the fertility chart Moon squared the natal Moon...not so good...but it fell in the 3rd house where it would conjunct the natal Sun, an ideal aspect for this type of Election. I suggested that she should not have intercourse until after 4:15 am (see Chart #27) at which time the Moon had advanced to 23 Capricorn 39, past the square to its natal position (23 Aries 31), but still applying to the sextile to Uranus and trine to Jupiter in the fertility chart.

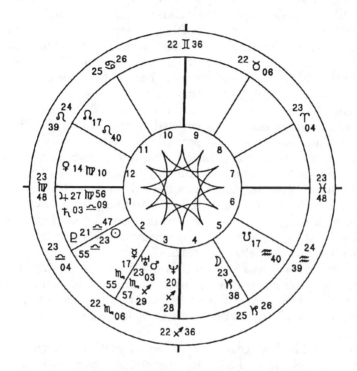

Example Chart #27
17 Oct 1980 at 4:15 am MET Monte Carlo, Monaco 43N45 7E25
Marissa — Fertility Chart #2

The other favorable date, if you wish to look at the chart, was December 15, 1980 at 1:52 am in Monte Carlo. We do not need to refer to it because she became pregnant on October 17, and yes, she had her period that day and the doctor to this day does not understand how it could possibly happen. I don't know the answer, but I have since urged many clients not to let anything stop them if they want to get pregnant. After all, it can't hurt and it may work. Marissa had a healthy baby girl, named Marion in my honor, on July 9, 1981.

In the 70s and early 80s I calculated many successful fertility charts, but in those simpler days, before complex conception methods became popular, or affordable, I also had some failures. Some clients came back two or three years in a row without successful results. I felt terrible for them and very inadequate for myself. Then one day (actually my first case was in 1984) a client wanted to know if I could help astrologically to assure an *in vitro* fertilization, since each time cost $10,000 and so far two *in vitro* attempts had failed to bring the desired results.

Pregnancies Through New Medical Procedures

What I have learned since 1984 is relatively uncomplicated. Most of the new methods such as *in vitro* or artificial insemination depend on dates given the patients by the doctor. In 95% of the cases I have dealt with, there is a 48-hour window where the patient can decide for herself when she wants to have the procedure done. This 48-hour period is the only time we, the astrologer, have to work with.

Obstetrics has become such a specialized field that most obstetricians work in pairs and are either located right next to the clinic they work with (not necessarily for giving birth, just for conception procedures) or have labs on the premises. This allows them to do whatever needs to be done at any time of the day or night. Most of my clients, none of whom were emergency cases, have given me a 14-hour day (from 6:00 am to 8:00 pm) to work with. In the 40-plus cases I have had thus far (again, not a great number as far as research goes, but enough to give food for thought), the closer the insemination was to the astrological fertility date, the better the results.

Several times I was able to convince my client to skip a month, realizing that her natural ovulation was moving toward the astrological peak day. This happens quite frequently, since many women ovulate every 27 or 28 days, while the astrological cycle is more or less 30 days.

I have also learned that when a client is totally out of sync with the astrological cycle and on a 30-day rhythm, in other words, no way of getting closer to the desired dates, then I do diurnal charts for the two or three days per month given me by the client and choose the best one. I do not try to find the best time for a particular day until the doctor actually orders my client to be ready (usually 24 hours notice), otherwise I would duplicate a lot of work, since every fertilization is different and does not take the same amount of time.

Another intriguing bit of learning came with the realization that it does not seem to matter when the eggs are taken from the ovaries or when the husband's sperm is added; it does not even matter when the eggs become fertile, the key moment is when the fertilized egg is implanted. This fact checks out time and time again.

In Vitro Fertilization

Take the case of Sarah — she had gone through a failed *in vitro* fertilization in February 1985. She was nearly 33 years old, depressed, panicky and $12,000 poorer. Her doctor said she could try again in April, May or June. The two days she gave me for April and May did not look as good as the ones for June 15-18.

Sarah was born April 10, 1952, at 8:31 am EST in Stamford, CT. Her chart is #28. She went to the clinic on June 15, 1985, at 7:30 am

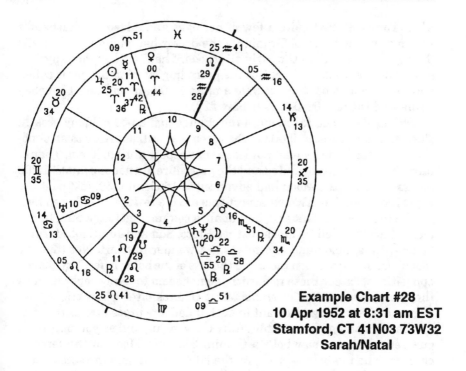

Example Chart #28
10 Apr 1952 at 8:31 am EST
Stamford, CT 41N03 73W32
Sarah/Natal

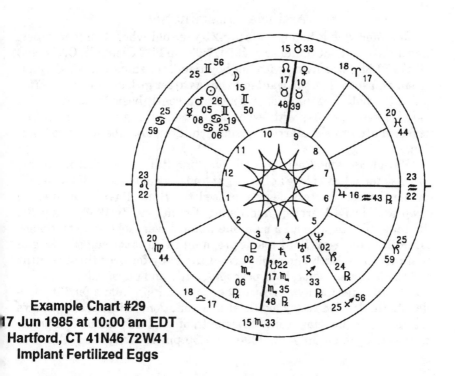

Example Chart #29
17 Jun 1985 at 10:00 am EDT
Hartford, CT 41N46 72W41
Implant Fertilized Eggs

EDT. They collected quite a few of her eggs and added her husband's sperm at about 12 noon. Originally the doctor had planned to implant the eggs on the 17th in the early afternoon. I had told her that anytime after 9:30 am would be fine. But the preceding evening the clinic called and asked her to be there at 9:00 am. At 10:00 am on June 17th they implanted the fertilized eggs (Chart #29).

When she called to tell me of the change in plans, I held my breath, since as you can see, at 9:00 am the Moon was still applying to an opposition of Uranus and would not leave that aspect until 9:30 am. Thankfully the Universe cooperated and the procedure did not start until 10:00 am and by then the Moon had advanced to 15 Gemini 50, just past the opposition. The Moon's next aspect was a trine to Jupiter followed by a sextile to the Ascendant and, best of all, a conjunction to the Sun. In her natal chart this Gemini Moon sextiled Pluto, Sun and Jupiter and trined her Neptune, Moon and Ascendant... a wonderful chart. Not that the Moon-Uranus opposition indicated the loss of the baby; in fertility charts, oppositions, except those to Saturn, do not seem to imply separation as they do by progression or transit. But Uranus often plays tricks, and that is the last thing you want in such a delicate procedure as *in vitro*.

Sarah's pregnancy was blissfully uneventful, and as you may have guessed when you saw both a Gemini Sun and Moon in the fertility chart, she had twin boys. One weighed 6 lbs. 10 oz. and the second one, born two minutes later, weighed 5 lbs. 6 oz.

Artificial Insemination

Jennifer was a happy-go-lucky 21-year-old when I first met her. (See natal chart #30 January 2, 1954, 7:09 pm PST Glendale, CA 34N08 118W15.) She was living with her boyfriend, finishing her college education and sure that she wanted to be "a career girl, all the way." After our initial natal consultation, we met on a yearly basis for updates and she also kept me busy with event charts concerning college tests. She never wanted to get married or have children and she had two abortions.

But along came Roberto, a good-looking Italian, as romantic as his name sounds. It was love at first sight and they married in 1984. Jennifer earned her masters degree, passed the State Boards and settled down to life as a Marriage and Family Counselor. By 1988, at age 34, she realized that without a baby she would never feel complete. Roberto felt the same way. She became pregnant twice at the end of 1988 and again in 1989. Each time she carried the baby for over three months and the loss was major, both psychologically and physically.

Finally, her family convinced her to seek help from a fertility specialist. He decided to try artificial insemination, using her husband's sperm and implanting it into the mouth of the birth canal. The procedure was done on July 12, 1990, at 2:30 pm in Hollywood, CA. (See

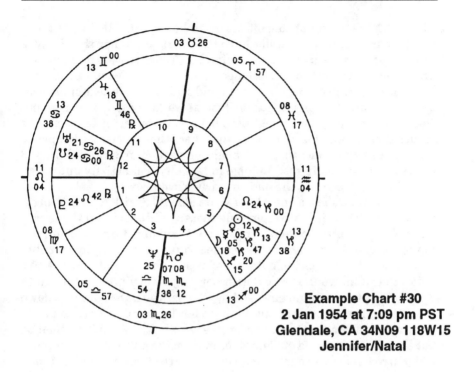

Example Chart #30
2 Jan 1954 at 7:09 pm PST
Glendale, CA 34N09 118W15
Jennifer/Natal

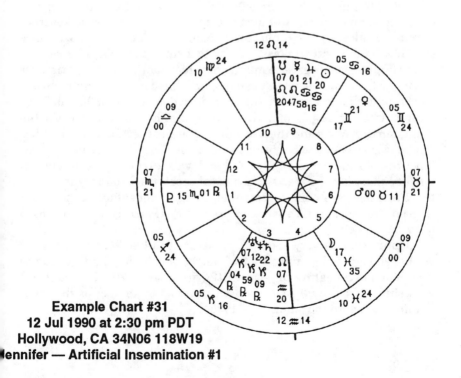

Example Chart #31
12 Jul 1990 at 2:30 pm PDT
Hollywood, CA 34N06 118W19
Jennifer — Artificial Insemination #1

Chart #31.) She did not consult me beforehand, but called right afterward for my opinion. I did not have the heart to tell her that I saw a problem around her usual danger point, between three and four months. The Moon in the 5th house applied to a square to Venus in the 8th house of surgery in 3¾ degrees. That could signify days, weeks or months, but with mutable signs (Moon in Pisces) we know it is not days but weeks, and in succedent (fixed sign) houses, we expect it to be months rather than weeks. I told her that since her other two losses happened around three plus months, she should be particularly careful around that time, to get more rest, indulge in less physical activity and so on. Unfortunately, she lost the baby in early November.

By this time she was nearly 37 years old and at risk for a first pregnancy. Her doctor initiated hormone therapy to strengthen the uterus and help prevent further miscarriages. He told her she could start trying again in July or August. We decided to run an astrological fertility cycle and see if any of the dates were close to her ovulation cycle. We found that if all went as calculated, her August ovulation would be 13 days off, September nine days and by October the difference was down to six days. November was out, because her husband was scheduled to be at a special training seminar for five weeks. It took a bit of cajoling, but since Jennifer could not afford too many more failures, neither physically, psychologically nor monetarily, she agreed to wait until October.

October 11th was the day and according to her doctor her appointment could be anywhere from 8:00 am to 10:00 pm. Since the preparations, including getting the husband's sperm, would take at least 45 minutes, I calculated the chart for 8:45 am PDT. (See chart #32.) Since the Moon at 3 Sagittarius is applying to a square to Venus (½ degree) and to Jupiter in 3 degrees equating to three months, a critical time for her in past pregnancies, I immediately informed her that under no circumstances should she have the procedure done before 3:00 pm. They inseminated her at 3:30 pm. (See chart #33.) The Moon will sextile the Sun, Mercury, Mars and the Ascendant. Natally the Moon falls into her 4th house very close to the 5th and will trine the natal Ascendant, conjunct the Moon, oppose Jupiter and end with a trine to Pluto. Though fertility chart lunar aspects to the natal chart are secondary in importance and are rarely life threatening, I was curious if anything would happen around the 12th week of pregnancy (Fertility Moon opposed natal Jupiter).

Jennifer had a very good pregnancy, but in her fourth month (12 weeks) she started gaining a lot of weight which she is still trying to lose. She had a healthy roly-poly little girl on June 26, 1992, and as I am writing this, she called for help with another pregnancy as she hopes to conceive before the summer of 1995.

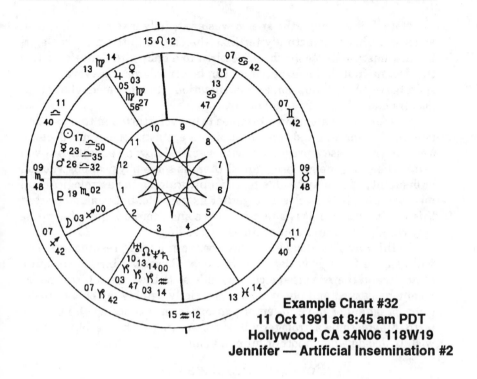

Example Chart #32
11 Oct 1991 at 8:45 am PDT
Hollywood, CA 34N06 118W19
Jennifer — Artificial Insemination #2

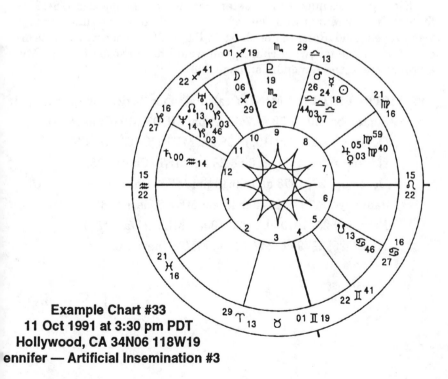

Example Chart #33
11 Oct 1991 at 3:30 pm PDT
Hollywood, CA 34N06 118W19
ennifer — Artificial Insemination #3

Note that although the sperm was artificially inseminated, it took at least 48 hours to actually fertilize the egg; despite an early Sagittarius (masculine) Moon, she gave birth to a baby girl. Jennifer asked the doctor what, in his experience, can be considered the average time span between insemination and fertilization. He confirmed what other doctors had told me, 24 to 60 hours.

The foregoing are a few examples to get you started in this exciting new field. Keep in mind that most of you are astrologers, not doctors. You can try to ease a pregnancy with so-called flowing aspects, but you cannot help anyone get pregnant if there is some physical obstruction or disability. You may be able to assist by bringing the astrological and medical procedure as closely together as possible, but remember that this is not a science. It is a non-intrusive and therefore quite harmless way of helping nature and at times succeeding.

In this day of medical advances, sooner or later I presume someone will ask me for a good day to give birth. Cæsarean births are quite common and there is often a choice made as to the time of birth. So far no one has asked and my expertise is strictly helping my clients to become pregnant. I have no empirical experience choosing the time of birth. Maybe some astrologer will start working with this, but I do not wish to decide when another human being should be born.

Fertility Practice Charts

Since practice makes the master, here is a seven month 1978-1979 fertility list for Mindy who wanted a second child by the time her boy was 2½ years old. Refer to her chart on Page 196 and see which date or dates, using the following charts, you would have chosen for her. My answers are in the Appendix on page 223.

FERTILITY LIST FOR MINDY calculated for Zurich, Switzerland

September 30, 1978 at 7:52:44 pm MEDT (-2) (Chart #34)

October 30, 1978 at 10:33:08 am MET (-1) (Chart #35)

November 29, 1978 at 0:56:28 am MET (Chart #36)

December 28, 1978 at 1:46:19 pm MET (Chart #37)

January 27, 1979 at 1:09:43 am MET (Chart #38)

February 25, 1979 at 11:22:40 am MET (Chart #39)

March 26, 1979 at 8:42:16 pm MET (Chart #40)

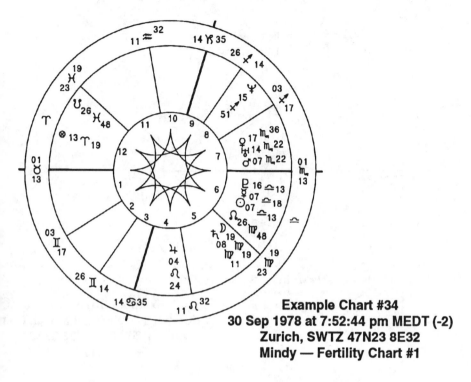

Example Chart #34
30 Sep 1978 at 7:52:44 pm MEDT (-2)
Zurich, SWTZ 47N23 8E32
Mindy — Fertility Chart #1

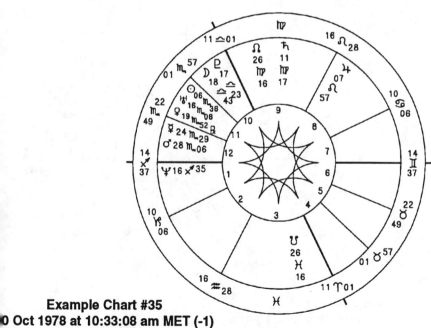

Example Chart #35
0 Oct 1978 at 10:33:08 am MET (-1)
Zurich, SWTZ 47N23 8E32
Mindy — Fertility Chart #2

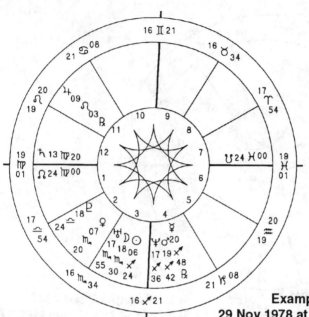

Example Chart #36
29 Nov 1978 at 00:56:28 am MET (-1
Zurich, SWTZ 47N23 8E32
Mindy — Fertility Chart #3

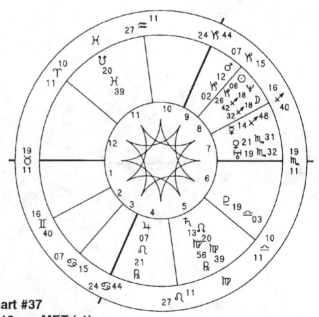

Example Chart #37
28 Dec 1978 at 1:46:19 pm MET (-1)
Zurich, SWTZ 47N23 8E32
Mindy — Fertility Chart #4

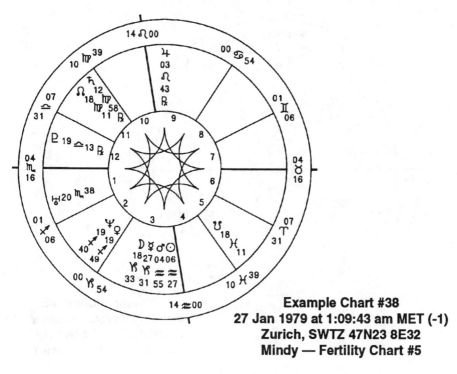

Example Chart #38
27 Jan 1979 at 1:09:43 am MET (-1)
Zurich, SWTZ 47N23 8E32
Mindy — Fertility Chart #5

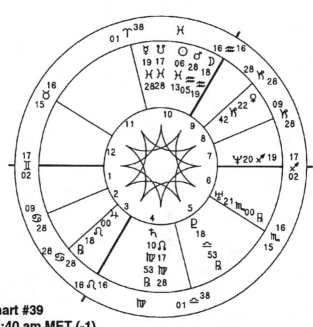

Example Chart #39
5 Feb 1979 at 11:22:40 am MET (-1)
Zurich, SWTZ 47N23 8E32
Mindy — Fertility Chart #6

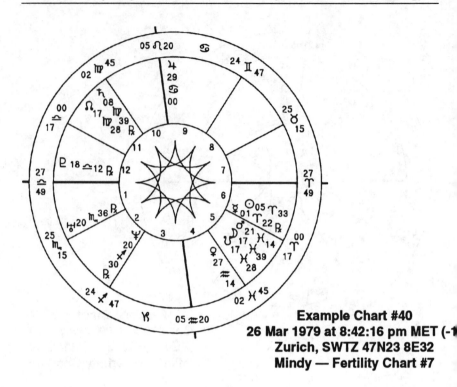

Example Chart #40
26 Mar 1979 at 8:42:16 pm MET (-1
Zurich, SWTZ 47N23 8E32
Mindy — Fertility Chart #7

LESSON XI

ODDS & ENDS

In working with so many charts, both Joan and I have come up with some ideas and concepts that have served us well over the years, so here are a few at random.

Many times people ask for an **Electional Chart** when a **Horary** would serve them much better, and vice versa. Help the client to think this out carefully. Take a lawsuit, for example; a Horary question: "Should I sue John Doe" will often give you a clearer answer than erecting an Electional Chart for when to sue him.

It is rarely wise to rely only on Electional or Horary charts and not check your natal, progressions, directions and transits to see what the natural flow of events is bringing. I do not mean relating your natal chart to the Electional or Horary one, but that it is necessary to move your horoscope forward to understand what is taking place.

As you may have noticed, I do not use the **Lunar Nodes** in Electional Astrology. That is neither good nor bad, and please feel free to use them if they help you. I have found that they do not add anything in this type of chart. So rather than clutter my chart with something I do not use, I eliminate them, but please do not confuse natal astrology, where the Nodes are extremely illuminating and revealing, with Electional Astrology.

The **Part of Fortune** is another astrological tool that I do not use consistently. But here the situation is reversed. I rarely use the Part of Fortune in natal astrology, but on occasion find it very handy for electional charting. As you may remember, the Moon is one of the most vital considerations and all the rules say that it should make a trine, sextile or friendly conjunction before leaving the sign. Sometimes, though, this is nearly impossible on a given day, and certain elections may call for a specific date. In such a case you can try to adjust the Ascendant until it results in a Part of Fortune that is trined, sextiled or conjuncted by the Moon before it goes void of course.

For example, assume the Moon is 23 Libra and its last aspect is a square to Mars at 25 Cancer, and the Sun is at 14 Leo. You should try for an Ascendant that's in the neighborhood of 18 Leo or later, in order to get a conjunction from the Moon to the Part of Fortune.

> **Ascendant 4 signs 18 degrees**
> **+   Moon 6 signs 23 degrees**
> **10 signs 41 degrees**
> **–   Sun 4 signs 14 degrees**
> **=   6 signs 27 degrees** or 27 Libra, which is past

the 25 degrees of Mars and the last aspect the Moon will make before leaving Libra is a conjunction to *Pars Fortuna*.

If this results in an unsuitable time or the planets fall in the wrong houses, you can try for a sextile by opting for a Part of Fortune in Leo or Sagittarius or a trine by putting the *Pars Fortuna* in Gemini or Aquarius.

Many years ago Joan thought it would make logical sense to file your Income Tax Return on a **Void of Course Moon**; after all, the void Moon is to be shunned because, supposedly, it will bring no action to whatever you try to do while it is in effect. In that case, Joan reasoned, if we mail our taxes under this so-called non-productive Moon, maybe you will not be audited. We cannot guarantee that it will work for you, but many of Joan's and my students, friends and relatives have tried it...and so far, so good.

As stated in the beginning of the Electional Astrology segment, the **natal chart** takes a back seat to the Electional chart, because the chart you "elect" becomes the birth chart of the event. To teach you the method, I featured only Electional charts. But that does not mean you should not look at the natal horoscope of the person for whom you are setting up an Electional Chart. Though not the most important, it often offers confirmation that you are on the right track. For instance, if you have two possible good times to open a business and one shows the Ascendant conjunct the client's Mercury, choose the one with the conjunction. In other words, when an Electional Chart has connections to the natal chart it serves as a verification; it somehow displays the synchronicity of the universe.

As you work with the many and diverse Electional Chart topics, please keep one thing in mind:

This is a method I have developed over many years. It works for me. Not all of it may work for you. Many of my colleagues use their own methodologies which work for them. None of us are right or wrong; we have tried different approaches and over the years perfected the one that is correct for us. That is what you, the reader, will eventually do. To start, you can use my ideas, concepts and suggestions. As you become more proficient, you will add your own touch and slowly but surely, what started as someone else's way will become your way, imbued with your logic, your language and your symbols. And that is as it should be.

PARTS OF CARS

(Thanks to Michael Munkasey)

1st house: Body, doors, driver's seat, front bumper and grill, horn, ignition system, starter and throttle.

2nd house: Dashboard padding, the seats and upholstery, the value retention.

3rd house: Connecting parts, distributor, fans, fan belt, fenders, fuel pump and hoses, the linkage, manifold, radio, steering system, tie rods, turn signals, the ventilation system, wheel rims.

4th house: Fuel lines, interior roominess, passenger seat, seat belts, undercoating, water hose and pump.

5th house: Chassis, combustion chamber, engine, engine block and mounts, headlights, motor, pistons.

6th house: Emission control system, fuel or oil filter, glove compartment, instrumentation, the jack, piston rings, preventive maintenance, repairs, spare tire, valve lifters.

7th house: Alignment, shock absorbers, springs, suspension system, torsion bars, windows, windshield, windshield wipers.

8th house: Exhaust system, muffler, radiator, voltage regulator.

9th house: Convertible top, fuel tank, oil pan, sun roof, universal joint.

10th house: Clutch, coolant, drive shaft, drive train, emergency brake, governor, transmission.

11th house: Air in tire, battery, carburetor, electrical system and wiring, exhaust header, fuel injectors, generator, hydraulic system, interior lights, mechanical linkages, power assist systems, valves.

12th house: Tires, trunk.

This list of automobile parts may prove helpful in questions when someone asks you what is wrong with their car.

ANSWERS TO HORARY TEST QUESTIONS

Answer to Test Chart #1. *"Should I build houses for and with Garrick?*

The querent is represented by the Moon at 27 Leo, Mars at 26 Cancer which is conjunct the Ascendant and Jupiter at 7 Leo in the 1st house. Garrick is ruled by Saturn at 6 Aquarius in and ruling the 7th. There is no aspect between the Moon and Saturn, Jupiter and Saturn or Mars and Saturn... all indicative of no action between the two men. Mars rules the 10th house of the querent's business and Mercury is in it at 4 Taurus. Mercury squares both Saturn and Jupiter, confirming a "no" answer and the void of course Moon also says that nothing will come of this.

Answer to Test Chart #2. *"Will Jerry get out on bail?"*

Jerry is the Moon at 24 Cancer in and ruling the 7th house (renumber the houses). He is also represented by the Sun in the 7th at 21 Cancer. Jupiter at 20 Taurus and Uranus at 28 Sagittarius are the planets of freedom and the Sun and Moon both sextile Jupiter (a "yes" answer), but they quincunx (changes) Uranus which rules his 8th house of money from outside sources (bail). He was released on bail, with the stipulation that his father have custody and take him out of the country. Mercury (ruler of his 12th) at 2 Cancer rules the 9th house (of foreign countries) and will conjunct the Sun.

Answer to Test Chart #3. *"Am I going to lose my home?"*

She is Mars at 19 Scorpio in the 12th, Pluto which is also there at 0 Scorpio as well as the Moon and Uranus at 7 and 12 Sagittarius respectively in the 1st house. Her home is depicted by Neptune, ruler of the 4th at 0 Capricorn. Mars makes no aspect to Neptune, nor does Uranus, so it looks like there will be no action. The Moon which co-rules the question, in this case rules her, by virtue of its 1st house position. It also makes no aspect to Neptune. Though there is a past (by minutes) sextile from Neptune to Pluto, this is not enough to contradict the lack of aspects by her rulers and does not really indicate the loss of her home. About three weeks after she asked the question she found a well-paying job and was able to hang on to the house.

Answer to Test Chart #4. *"Will Pete get his truck back?"*

First, **renumber the chart.** Pete is the 7th house ruled by Mercury at 9 Virgo in his 3rd of automobiles (a valid question). For all questions pertaining to cars I use the 3rd house and Mercury which rules it in the flat chart. Mercury is dignified in Virgo, so things look promising. It also will conjunct the Sun which rules the 3rd at 23 Virgo in that house. With any lost item question, it is advisable to analyze the ruler of the 2nd, which in this case means co-ruler of the question, the Moon. The Moon at 4 Capricorn is in the house of the thief (Pete's 7th) and trines Mercury and the Sun. But it also conjuncts Uranus and Neptune. The answer is "yes" he will get it back but not the way it was. Whenever Uranus is involved in a lost item question, the object is not returned in the same condition, usually worse. With Mars in the 3rd house, it seemed that the police might have a hand in the return.

Twelve days later the police called and reported that they had found the truck. No wheels, no battery and everything was disconnected to lift the engine, but they must have been interrupted. My clients were out their deductible, but got the truck back.

Answer to Test Chart #5. *"Is Matt guilty of the hit-and-run accident?"*

Turn the chart or renumber to make the 7th house number 1. The Sun at 27 Gemini and Venus at 12 Leo represent Matt. Accidents are ruled by Uranus and Mars and are the province of the 3rd house. Venus rules his 3rd; Uranus is in it. Mars is in his 9th (the 3rd of the chart). Venus trines Mars and sextiles Uranus. The Sun trines Uranus but is past the sextile to Mars. The "yes" answers win. The chart says he is guilty.

Matt maintained his innocence until he went to court and lost and went to prison for involuntary manslaughter.

Answer to Test Chart #6. *"Will the insurance company sue me? If so, will they win?"*

My client is represented by Jupiter at 8 Cancer, ruler of the Ascendant in the 8th house. A valid chart considering that her concern was about a possible debt. Any adversary is found in the 7th house, so Mercury at 7 Libra rules the insurance company. Mercury squares Jupiter indicating "no" they will not sue her. The Moon at 27 Taurus is Void of Course, confirmation that nothing will happen. It didn't.

Answer to Test Chart #7. *"Will my daughter-in-law be involved in a lawsuit?"*

You must first renumber the houses or turn the chart so the 11th house is on the Ascendant. Her son is the 5th, his wife is the 11th, thus the Moon at 3 Virgo represents the daughter-in-law; so does Jupiter at 4 Leo which is in her 1st house... a valid question since Jupiter rules legal situations. Saturn at 6 Aquarius rules and is in the 5th (her 7th house) which depicts lawsuits. The Moon quincunxes Saturn and Jupiter opposes it, indicating a "no" (opposition), or that something would have to change (quincunx). The case was settled out of court and she never had to appear.

Answer to Test Chart #8: *"Should I hire Gretel?"*

The querent is ruled by Neptune at 16 Capricorn in the 11th. Gretel is represented by the 7th house, ruler by Mercury at 4 Libra in the 7th. Mercury squares Neptune indicating a "no" answer.

Answer to Test Chart #9. *"Should we buy the Osburn property?"*

Venus at almost 22 Cancer rules the querent and the 4th house denotes property. It is ruled by the Moon at 18 Libra. The Moon squares Venus; the answer is "no."

Answer to Test Chart #10. *"Where is the headache medicine?"*

Saturn rules the 2nd house identifying the lost item. It is in the 12th at 9 Sagittarius, indicating it is near heat (fire sign) and hidden in an enclosed place like a cupboard or closet (12th). Uranus at 20 Sagittarius is the co-ruler of the 2nd house (Aquarius intercepted) and is also in the 12th. Jupiter at 13 Pisces in the 3rd disposits both Saturn and Uranus. Venus, the dispositor of the Part of Fortune is at 7 Scorpio in the 10th. Water signs suggest bathroom, laundry or kitchen. Sagittarius is high. She found the medication in a high cupboard in the kitchen. The cabinets backs onto a gas heater.

ANSWERS TO ELECTIONAL TEST QUESTIONS

Mindy's timing was excellent. There were more "good" and "okay" dates than I usually encounter in a seven month period.

Chart #34: September 30, 1978 7:52 pm MEDT, Zurich, Switzerland

The Moon, though at only 19 Virgo, is void of course. I suggested that they try a few hours earlier, around 3:00 pm, in order to catch the sextile to Venus at 17 Scorpio, yet avoid the square to Neptune at nearly 16 Sagittarius. They did, but nothing happened. I have noticed this phenomenon a few times whenever the fertility chart ends with a void of course Moon regardless of how we adjust the time of intercourse. All of this is still experimental from my viewpoint and I am not yet prepared to definitely state that a VOC Moon prohibits a successful pregnancy.

Chart #35: October 30, 1978 10:33 am MET Zurich, Switzerland

The Moon at 18 Libra is void of course and again I suggested an earlier try at about 8:00 am to capitalize on the sextile to Neptune and particularly the conjunction to Pluto, which I have found to be beneficial when it comes to reproduction of any kind. Again, no pregnancy, but they had fun practicing.

Chart #36: November 29, 1978 12:56 am MET Zurich, Switzerland

The Moon at 18 Scorpio was again void of course, but first it sextiled the Ascendant. I suggested trying a half hour earlier to take advantage of the sextile to Pluto, yet avoid the conjunction to Uranus as the Moon's first applying aspect. I needn't have worried...her husband was out of town.

Chart #37: December 28, 1978 1:46 pm MET Zurich, Switzerland

I liked this chart which ends with a lunar sextile to Pluto, although the Moon's first applying aspect, a conjunction to Neptune had fooled me before and did it again. Neptune's elusive quality seems to manifest as wishful thinking...because Mindy did not get pregnant.

Chart #38: January 27, 1979 1:09 am MET Zurich, Switzerland

The Moon at 18 Capricorn squared Pluto and though I like Pluto in pregnancy charts, I felt a square was a bit risky. Since the sextile to Uranus (ruling the Sun here) and the conjunction to Mercury were positive, I counseled them to wait until 2:45 am. She became pregnant and had a lovely little girl on October 12, 1979. Her Cancer Moon conjuncts her brother's Cancer Sun.

It is lucky that Mindy got pregnant in January, because neither Chart #39 or #40 looked very promising. In #39 the Moon begins with a trine to Pluto, also the Ascendant if we start a bit earlier, but then there is a square to Uranus, a definite "no." Chart #40 is not much better with a quincunx to Pluto and a trine to Uranus, followed by a square to Neptune, another "no."

HOW to Order a
Basic Natal Chart

The publisher of this book offers a **Chart Service**
whereby you can order a Basic Natal Chart.

We suggest our 4-color Student Chart for only $5 because,
you don't have to know how to read astrological glyphs —
the positions are given in words, too.

There is a $2 postage and handling charge per order.

Call Toll Free
1-800-888-9983

Monday - Friday, 9AM to 5PM Pacific Time
We accept MasterCard, VISA and AMEX

OR

Send your check or money order for $7.00
with your place of birth (city & state), date of birth
and time of birth (hour & minute and AM/PM) to:

ACS Publications
PO Box 34487, Dept. OWH94
San Diego, CA 92163-4487

Survey

What were your two highest expectations
of *Volume VI* of *The Only Way... Series?*

1. _____

_____

_____

_____

2. _____

_____

_____

_____

How well did we fulfill those expectations?

_____

_____

_____

_____

_____

_____

_____